THE·EVERYDAY·TURKEY·COOKBOOK

THE·EVERYDAY·TURKEY·COOKBOOK

Franki Papai Secunda

Illustrations by
Michelle Burchard

HPBooks

HPBooks
Published by the Penguin Group
Penguin Group (USA) Inc.
375 Hudson Street, New York, New York 10014, USA
Penguin Group (Canada), 10 Alcorn Avenue, Toronto, Ontario M4V 3B2, Canada
(a division of Pearson Penguin Canada Inc.)
Penguin Books Ltd., 80 Strand, London WC2R 0RL, England
Penguin Group Ireland, 25 St. Stephen's Green, Dublin 2, Ireland (a division of Penguin Books Ltd.)
Penguin Group (Australia), 250 Camberwell Road, Camberwell, Victoria 3124, Australia
(a division of Pearson Australia Group Pty. Ltd.)
Penguin Books India Pvt. Ltd., 11 Community Centre, Panchsheel Park, New Delhi—110 017, India
Penguin Group (NZ), Cnr. Airborne and Rosedale Roads, Albany, Auckland 1310, New Zealand
(a division of Pearson New Zealand Ltd.)
Penguin Books (South Africa) (Pty.) Ltd., 24 Sturdee Avenue, Rosebank, Johannesburg 2196, South
Africa

Penguin Books Ltd., Registered Offices: 80 Strand, London WC2R 0RL, England

PRINTING HISTORY
First HP trade paperback edition / November 1995

HPBooks is a registered trademark of Penguin Group (USA) Inc.
The "HPBooks" design is a trademark belonging to Penguin Group (USA) Inc.

ISBN: 1-55788-443-9

Library of Congress Cataloging-in-Publication Information

Secunda, Franki Papai.
    The everyday turkey cookbook / Franki Papai Secunda.—1st ed.
        p.   cm.
    ISBN 1-55788-219-3 (pbk. : acid-free paper)
    1. Cookery (Turkey)   I. Title
TX750.5.T87S43   1995
641.6'6592—dc20   95-8127

PRINTED IN THE UNITED STATES OF AMERICA

10   9   8   7   6   5   4   3

I dedicate this book in memory of my very best friend, my husband and partner, Tony Secunda. Yea, T. S., we did it!

Acknowledgments

A very special thank-you to my friends in the research and development department, also known as official taste testers, who were subject to my endless experimentations and last-minute dinner invitations. They include Tom Sheridan, Sue Meherin, Linda Kelly, Bud Johnson, and Terrie and George Pagan. Special thanks to Crisco Janda, Tokyo Joe and Linda McGovern for their Joe-Linda's Barbecue Turkey; Nikki Mitchell, who contributed her fabulous Nikki's Texas Turkey Chili; Beverly Dubin, who was the original fan of the Tuesday Night Dinosaur–Turkey Leg Club; Jane's truckstop special; Grandma and Grandpa Papai; Roxy and Rocket Secunda, and my husband, Tony, who stood by me in the longest hours of this project, and was the chief and official taste tester.

Contents

Foreword

Turkey is a meat surprising Americans today with its versatility, nutrition and economy. Turkey meat is appearing in an ever-expanding variety of light and dark meat cuts. It is a naturally mild meat that is readily enhanced by flavoring ingredients. Today's aware consumers are finding that products such as ground turkey, turkey breast cutlets, steaks and tenderloins work easily in their favorite traditional recipes. Then there is the whole array of fully cooked turkey products, such as turkey ham, bologna, pastrami and smoked turkey breast, that make meal preparation a breeze.

Turkey meat has a proven low percentage of fat, especially saturated fat, and is very high in protein. A three-ounce cooked serving has only one gram of fat and 119 calories.

The economy of turkey meat is due in part to its sizable cuts, with an excellent meat-to-bone ratio. Meat is derived from thighs and breasts of today's specially bred turkeys, many of which weigh well over thirty pounds. Processed much like beef or veal, raw meat cuts are perfect for stews, pot roast, sautés, stir-fries and barbecues. Low-fat turkey dark meats are tasty twins to their red meat counterparts.

The prime factor in the versatility of turkey meat is its flavor compatibility with other foods. It's astounding how readily turkey takes on character from hearty sauces and spices. In fact, turkey is a delicious substitute in any of your family's favorite recipes. For instance, turkey thigh meat is fabulous in turkey ragout or stew. And, turkey cutlets are perfect in traditional veal recipes . . . as any good chef will attest.

Turkey is no longer reserved just for Thanksgiving. It is truly a year-round favorite. Our industry is proud of the progress we have made to make turkey products available to the world.

Cookbooks, such as this one featuring the many ways to serve turkey, are an excellent means to make consumers aware of interesting ways to prepare our favorite bird.

Kenneth D. Rutledge, Chairman
National Turkey Federation

Introduction

The delights of turkey are no longer reserved for Thanksgiving and Christmas. Over the last twenty years, turkey has made an amazing impact here in the United States and it is now one of America's fastest-growing exports. Turkey can be prepared in many different ways and it can also be the basis for healthy eating. Of all the popular meats, turkey is one of the lowest in fat and cholesterol content.

These days all the supermarkets have turkey cuts of every kind; there are turkey cutlets, turkey breast roasts, breast medallions, tenderloins, steaks, drumsticks, thighs, and wings and even ground turkey. In addition to fresh turkey products, processed turkey is made into turkey hams, turkey sausages and turkey bacons. The selection is available year-round, too.

In this book you will find a variety of preparation methods for your turkey, from turkey parts to the whole bird. Whatever your preference, this book will give you the most comprehensive collection of recipes to enjoy this famous bird.

Handle Your Turkey With Care

The most important preparation tip to remember before and after cooking your turkey is to handle your turkey with care. The steps listed below will help you have a safe, simple, and fabulous meal without all the worries. The rest is easy, just follow the recipes for some of the best turkey meals ever.

Buying Turkey

When buying your turkey, make sure you get the right weight bird so that you have enough to feed everyone. Generally it's a pound of raw turkey per person; this allows for a moderate amount of leftovers. If you purchase a frozen turkey, allow enough time for thawing (see below). If the turkey has a date listed on the wrapper, use it before the date listed, especially if the turkey is fresh.

Avoid fresh turkeys that are stored above the top of the supermarket's refrigeration case. Remember bacteria thrive above 40° Fahrenheit.

Storing Turkey

To store your fresh turkey, make sure it's in the original wrapper. Fresh turkeys should be stored at 40° Fahrenheit or below. Fresh turkeys should be stored in the coldest part of the refrigerator for no more than two days before cooking them.

Freezing Fresh Turkey

Most fresh turkeys can be safely frozen in their original wrappers for up to two months. If you want to freeze your turkey for a longer period, you'll need to rewrap your turkey.

Follow these easy steps: (1) Remove the giblets from the cavity of the turkey and remove them from the bag. Rinse the giblets under cold running water and pat dry with paper towels. Place in a plastic freezer bag. Label, date, and freeze. (2) Trim any excess fat from the whole turkey. Tightly wrap the turkey using freezer-strength plastic, paper, or foil. Label, date, and freeze. You can freeze a rewrapped whole turkey for up to one year. (3) Cut-up turkey pieces such as breasts and tenderloins can be frozen up to three months. Larger cuts such as drumsticks and thighs with skin can be frozen for six months. Again, wrap these turkey parts properly, label, date, and freeze.

Thawing Frozen Turkey

To thaw your frozen turkey follow these easy steps: (1) For a whole turkey, place the wrapped turkey on a tray in the refrigerator. Allow 5 hours per pound to thaw completely. If time is short, place the wrapped turkey in the sink and cover with cold water. Allow 1-1/2 hours per pound for the turkey to thaw completely. Change the water every 30 minutes. Never thaw turkey at room temperature, as it promotes bacterial growth. To thaw turkey parts as a general rule, place them in your refrigerator for 24 hours. If you are in a hurry, follow the manufacturer's instructions for thawing turkey parts in a microwave oven.

Kitchen Safety

Before handling your turkey, make sure your cutting board, utensils, your hands, and the area you are working in are clean. Wear kitchen gloves if you have abrasions or cuts on your hands. Remove the giblets and neck and rinse turkey inside and out with cold water. Pat the turkey dry with paper towels inside and out as well. Wash your hands and all surfaces that have come in contact with the raw turkey with soap and hot water.

Stuffing

If you are stuffing your turkey, loosely stuff the turkey with cool stuffing just before placing it in the oven. One cup of stuffing per pound of turkey is the general rule. Never stuff the turkey ahead of time. The cooked stuffing should reach a temperature of 165°F (75°C). Remove stuffing as soon as the bird is cooked. Refrigerate leftover stuffing separately.

Cooking Whole Turkeys

Cook turkey in a 325°F (165°C) oven; do not use a lower oven temperature or the turkey will cook too slowly and allow bacteria to grow.

Use a meat thermometer to determine doneness. Place the thermometer in the thickest part of your turkey, usually the inner thigh, without touching the bone.

Loosely place a foil tent over the top of the turkey. To let the turkey brown evenly all over, remove foil for the last hour of cooking. Do not place a tight-fitting lid over the turkey and do not cover the entire turkey with foil or your turkey will taste steamed instead of roasted.

When your thermometer reads 180°F (80°C), or 170°F (75°C) if thermometer is placed in the breast, your turkey is done. When the thigh is pierced with a fork the juices should run clear. Make sure your turkey is always cooked completely before eating. Never cook turkey partially and then store it to be finished later. For more detailed roasting techniques, see page 72.

Cooking Turkey Parts

Use a fork to test bone-in turkey parts; a fork inserted into the meat should go in with ease and the juices should run clear. The meat and juices nearest the bone may still be a little pink even though the turkey is cooked thoroughly. However, the meat should no longer be pink in the center. Boneless turkey pieces are done when the centers are no longer pink; test this by cutting into the centers with a knife.

Storing Leftover Turkey

After your meal, the turkey, stuffing, and gravy should not stand at room temperature for more than 2 hours or bacteria will multiply to dangerous levels.

Remove the meat from the carcass, place the meat in covered containers, and refrigerate the carcass for making turkey stock. You may need several covered containers for the meat. Store the stuffing and the gravy in separate covered containers, and store all of these containers in the coldest part of the refrigerator. Leftover turkey will keep in the refrigerator for three to four days; stuffing and gravy should be used within two days.

To freeze leftover turkey, place the meat in freezer wrap, plastic freezer bags, or plastic freezer containers. Label, date, and freeze. To freeze stuffing and gravy, place in a vaporproof container. Label, date, and freeze. Frozen leftover turkey, stuffing, and gravy should be used within one month. Thaw frozen leftovers overnight in the refrigerator or in a microwave oven.

Soups for Every Occasion

I remember as a child the bowl of hot soup that would cure what ailed you. Once eaten, the soup would make you forget just about everything that was wrong.

These days I love to cook homemade soups and stews. It makes me feel good just to put all of those magic ingredients into one pot. In this chapter there are turkey soups that can be served either hot or cold. There is an easy and delightful stock that is good for soups, as well as for all kinds of gravies and many entrées.

For those cold winter nights, there is tasty Bean & Turkey Soup and Hearty Turkey Stew, both meals in themselves. There are light soups such as Turkey & Cucumber Soup and Chilled Curried Turkey Soup.

Turkey soups are easy to make, and also rewarding. So make some turkey soup today—it's a natural cure for everything from the sniffles to the winter blahs.

Turkey Stock

This is a basic turkey stock that is excellent for your soups, gravies, and tasty stews. I refer to this recipe a lot, so when I say turkey stock, this is the one. I often make enough to freeze. The real secret to making your broth is to never let it come to a boil. To enhance the flavor, I add some canned chicken broth. My grandmother would add a couple of chicken wings to her turkey broth as well, that was her secret.

Carcass from 1 (10- to 16-pound) cooked turkey, broken up
2 quarts water
1 (8-ounce) can chicken broth or 1 chicken bouillon cube dissolved in 1 cup hot water
1/2 cup white wine (optional)
1 large onion
1 medium-size leek, white part only, chopped

2 celery stalks, quartered
1 carrot, quartered
3 parsley sprigs
Freshly cracked pepper to taste
1 bay leaf
1 teaspoon dried thyme
2 chicken wings (optional)

In a large, heavy pot, add all the ingredients. Bring to a simmer over medium-high heat. Skim off the foam and reduce heat to low.

Simmer 2 to 3 hours or longer. Turn off heat and let stand about 15 minutes. The fat will rise to the top. Remove fat with a large spoon and discard. Strain the broth. Use immediately in soups, stews, or gravies. Or refrigerate or freeze the broth for later use. Makes about 2-1/2 quarts (8 cups).

Turkey Consommé

The word consommé *comes from the French word meaning "to boil down."*
It is a strong soup made by reducing the broth, then clarifying it to make it sparkling clear.
Perfect for any formal meal.

1 recipe Turkey Stock (see opposite)   2 shells from the egg whites, crushed
2 egg whites

Reduce stock by boiling uncovered to one half its original volume. For each quart of consommé, place egg whites and their crushed shells in a medium-size bowl. Beat until frothy and about double their original volume. Pour egg whites and shells into consommé and bring back to a boil, stirring constantly. Turn off heat. Allow to rest about 10 minutes. This will allow the egg whites and shells to rise to the top and collect all the particles (any particles will cling to the shells).

Line a wire strainer with a damp layer of muslin or cheesecloth. Place strainer over a large bowl. Gently ladle consommé into the strainer. The consommé will slowly drip through the cloth and will be clear. Reheat consommé and serve immediately or refrigerate or freeze for later use. Makes 4 to 6 servings.

Variation

Jellied Consommé

Follow directions above. Place the bowl of consommé in the refrigerator and chill until jellied. Cut into small cubes. Serve on a bed of lettuce and garnish with parsley or watercress sprigs.

Bean & Turkey Soup

This soup is chock-full of goodies. It's great to have some leftover, because you can just take it out of the refrigerator the next day and warm it up for a quick and easy meal.

1-1/2 cups mixed dried beans, preferably as
    many different beans as possible, soaked
    overnight
2 tablespoons olive oil
1 large onion, chopped
2 large garlic cloves, crushed
1 cup medium-size green bell pepper, chopped
1 cup chopped celery

1 cup chopped carrot
1 cup chopped cooked turkey
1 bay leaf
Salt and pepper to taste
1/2 teaspoon dried Italian seasoning
1 teaspoon dried basil
1 (16-ounce) can Italian-style stewed tomatoes

Add beans and enough water to cover to a large pot. Boil 10 minutes. Reduce heat, cover, and simmer 1-1/2 hours.

In a large skillet, heat oil. Add onion, garlic, bell pepper, celery, and carrot, and cook until vegetables are tender. Drain beans and add vegetables, turkey, bay leaf, salt, pepper, Italian seasoning, basil, and tomatoes. Cover with water. Simmer 1 hour or until beans are tender. Makes about 8 or 9 servings.

Corn & Turkey Chowder

My friend Sue from Chicago said that the soup section wouldn't be complete without this recipe.
Instead of using regular bacon, her family uses turkey bacon. So here it is—their secret recipe.

4 slices turkey bacon
1 cup chopped onion
2 cups cubed potatoes
2 cups Turkey Stock (page 2) or
   1 (15-1/4-ounce) can chicken broth
2 cups diced cooked turkey

1 (8-ounce) can whole-kernel corn, drained
1 (8-ounce) can cream-style corn
1 cup half-and-half
1/4 teaspoon freshly cracked pepper
1/2 teaspoon dried basil
Chopped fresh parsley

In a medium-size skillet, fry turkey bacon until crisp. Drain on paper towels, then crumble. Add onion to skillet and cook, stirring occasionally, until tender, about 10 minutes. In a Dutch oven, combine onion, potatoes, and stock, and bring to a boil. Reduce heat, cover, and simmer until potatoes are tender, about 15 minutes. Add turkey, whole corn, creamed corn, half-and-half, pepper, and basil. Heat thoroughly. Garnish each serving with the crumbled turkey bacon and chopped parsley. Makes 4 to 6 servings.

Easy Turkey Gumbo

The word gumbo *comes from the African word* gombo, *which means "okra."*
There are as many versions of gumbo as there are cooks on the bayous.
This is a simple version that uses leftover turkey. Enjoy.

1 tablespoon butter
1 onion, finely chopped
1/2 cup chopped celery
4 cups Turkey Stock (page 2) or
   2 (15-1/4-ounce) cans chicken broth
1/2 green bell pepper, finely chopped

1 cup chopped fresh or frozen okra
1/2 cup chopped cooked turkey
1 teaspoon salt
1/2 teaspoon ground white pepper
1 (16-ounce) can tomatoes, chopped
Cooked rice

Melt butter in a large skillet over medium heat. Add onion and celery, and cook about 6 minutes or until softened, stirring constantly. Add stock, bell pepper, okra, turkey, salt, pepper, and tomatoes, and bring to a boil. Reduce heat, cover, and simmer about 45 minutes. Serve over cooked rice. Makes 4 servings.

Turkey Parmigiana Soup

An Italian soup made with zucchini or yellow squash and shredded mozzarella cheese.
A meal in itself.

3 cups water
1 cup Turkey Stock (page 2) or chicken broth
1 cup chopped fresh tomatoes or 1 (8-ounce) can tomatoes
1/2 pound turkey cutlets, cut into 1/2-inch cubes

1/2 teaspoon dried oregano
1/2 teaspoon garlic powder
1/2 teaspoon dried basil
1 cup sliced zucchini or yellow squash
1/3 cup shredded mozzarella cheese
Freshly grated Parmesan cheese to taste

In a large saucepan, combine all ingredients except the cheeses and bring to a boil. Reduce heat to low, cover, and simmer, stirring occasionally, about 8 minutes, or until turkey is no longer pink in center. Spoon into bowls; sprinkle with mozzarella and Parmesan cheeses. Makes about 5 servings.

Indian Summer Turkey Soup

We like to make this during the hot days of summer, because it doesn't take very long to prepare.
It's so nice not to have to turn on the oven when it's hot.

4 cups water
1 cup Turkey Stock (page 2) or chicken broth
1/2 pound cooked turkey, diced
1 small tomato, diced

1/2 cup diagonally cut canned asparagus pieces
1 (10-ounce) can whole-kernel corn, undrained
1/4 teaspoon fennel seeds, crushed

In a large saucepan, bring water to a boil over medium heat. Stir in remaining ingredients. Return to a boil, reduce heat to low, and simmer, uncovered, about 10 minutes. Serve hot. Makes 6 servings.

Mulligatawny Turkey Soup

This classic originated in India. Now you can make this delightfully rich soup in your own home.
Serve with rice for a complete meal.

3 medium-size carrots, peeled and sliced
2 stalks celery, sliced
6 cups Turkey Stock (page 2) or chicken broth
3 cups chopped cooked turkey
1/4 cup butter or margarine
1 cup chopped onion
1 apple, peeled, quartered, cored, and
   chopped

5 teaspoons curry powder
1 teaspoon salt, or to taste
1/4 cup all-purpose flour
1 tablespoon fresh lemon juice
2 cups cooked rice
6 lemon slices
6 parsley sprigs

In a medium-size saucepan, cook carrots and celery in 1 cup of the stock 20 minutes or until vegetables are tender. Add turkey; heat just until hot, cover, and keep warm.

Melt butter in a Dutch oven over medium heat. Add onion and cook until soft. Stir in apple, curry powder, and salt, and cook about 5 minutes longer, or until apple is soft. Add flour, gradually stir in remaining stock, and heat to boiling, stirring constantly. Reduce heat, cover, and simmer 15 minutes. Add vegetables and turkey with cooking liquid and bring just to a boil. Stir in lemon juice.

To serve, put 2 heaping spoonfuls of hot cooked rice into large individual soup bowls, ladle soup over rice, and garnish with a lemon slice and a parsley sprig. Makes 6 servings.

Chilled Curried Turkey Soup

This soup is best as a starter on a hot evening. It's one of my favorite cold soups, I'm sure you'll agree.

1 tablespoon butter or margarine
3 tart apples, peeled, cored, sliced
1 large onion, sliced
2 teaspoons curry powder
Salt and freshly ground pepper to taste
3 drops hot sauce

3 cups Turkey Consommé (page 3) or chicken broth
1 cup dry white wine
1 cup half-and-half
1/2 cup finely diced cooked turkey
Paprika

Melt butter in a large saucepan over low heat. Add apples and onion, and cook, stirring often, until they are soft. Do not let apples and onion brown. Stir in curry powder and cook 3 minutes longer. Add salt and pepper, hot sauce, consommé, and wine. Cover and simmer 10 minutes, stirring often.

Transfer apple mixture to a blender or food processor and process until pureed. Pour into a large bowl, cover, and refrigerate until completely chilled. Just before serving, stir in half-and-half and turkey. Sprinkle with paprika. Serve chilled. Makes 6 servings.

Turkey & Cucumber Soup

Here's a fresh crunchy soup that's quick to prepare. Make sure that the cucumbers
are not bitter by tasting them first. If the cucumbers are bitter, sprinkle the slices with salt,
let stand 30 minutes, then rinse well before using.

2 cucumbers, peeled
4 cups Turkey Stock (page 2) or chicken broth
1 cup finely chopped cooked turkey

3 tablespoons sherry
Sour cream
Fresh dill weed

Cut each cucumber in half lengthwise and remove seeds with a spoon; discard seeds. Cut cucumbers into thin slices. In a large saucepan, bring stock to a boil; reduce heat to low. Add turkey and cucumbers, and simmer 15 minutes. Add sherry. Ladle soup into bowls. Top each serving with a dollop of sour cream and lightly sprinkle with dill weed. Makes 4 to 6 servings.

Hearty Turkey Stew

This stew is great on cold winter nights. It's a full-course meal.
Serve with hot biscuits so that no one misses a drop of the delicious gravy.

3 tablespoons olive oil
5 medium-size carrots, peeled and chopped
1 large onion, chopped
1 pound uncooked turkey breast, cut into 1-inch
    strips
1 teaspoon garlic powder
1/2 teaspoon dried parsley
3 tablespoons all-purpose flour

8 small red potatoes, cut into 1/2-inch cubes
1 cup sliced mushrooms
1 cup Turkey Stock (page 2) or chicken broth
1 (8-ounce) can tomato sauce
1/2 tablespoon chili powder
1 teaspoon ground cumin
1/2 tablespoon paprika

Preheat oven to 350°F (175°C). In a large skillet, heat olive oil over medium heat. Add carrots and onion, and cook until vegetables are tender. Add turkey strips, garlic powder, and parsley, and cook 3 minutes, or until turkey is lightly browned. Stir in flour. Pour mixture into a 3-quart casserole dish. Add potatoes, mushrooms, stock, tomato sauce, chili powder, cumin, and paprika.

Bake 45 minutes, or until potatoes are tender and turkey is no longer pink in center. Let stand 5 minutes before serving. Makes 8 to 10 servings.

Turkey Thigh Ragout in Crust

A fabulous stew with a pastry topping, with each serving in its own small casserole dish.
The stew has olives, small onions, a red potato, snow peas, and herbs in a delicious gravy.
It's the perfect dish for a dinner for two.

1 tablespoon vegetable oil
2 turkey thighs, skinned, boned, and cut into
   1-inch cubes
2 garlic cloves, minced
1/4 cup thinly sliced mushrooms
1/4 cup boiling onions, skins removed
1 medium-size red potato, cut into 1/2-inch
   cubes
1/2 cup Turkey Stock (page 2) or chicken broth

1/2 teaspoon minced fresh parsley
1/8 teaspoon dried thyme
1 small bay leaf
1/3 cup snow peas (about 10)
1/4 cup chopped ripe olives
1 (4-ounce) can refrigerator crescent rolls
1 egg yolk beaten with 1 teaspoon water
1/2 teaspoon dried dill weed

Preheat oven to 375°F (190°C). Heat oil in a medium-size skillet over medium heat. Add turkey cubes, garlic, and mushrooms, and cook about 5 minutes or until the turkey is no longer pink in the center when cut with a knife. Remove the turkey, mushrooms, and garlic, and set aside.

Add onions and cook until onions are lightly browned. Add potato, stock, parsley, thyme, and bay leaf, and bring mixture to a boil. Reduce heat, cover, and simmer 10 minutes or until potato is tender. Remove and discard bay leaf. Add turkey mixture, snow peas, and olives. Divide the mixture between 2 (1-3/4-cup) casserole dishes.

Divide crescent roll into 2 rectangles and press seams together. Roll out each rectangle to make dough large enough to cover top of casserole dishes. Cut a small decorative shape out of the center to let steam escape. Place dough over casseroles; trim to fit. Press dough to edges of each casserole to seal. Brush with egg yolk mixture and sprinkle with dill weed.

Bake 8 minutes or until dough is golden brown. Makes 2 servings.

Variation

For a lattice crust, cut each rectangle into 6 lengthwise strips. Arrange strips, lattice fashion, over each casserole; press ends of dough to edges of each casserole to seal.

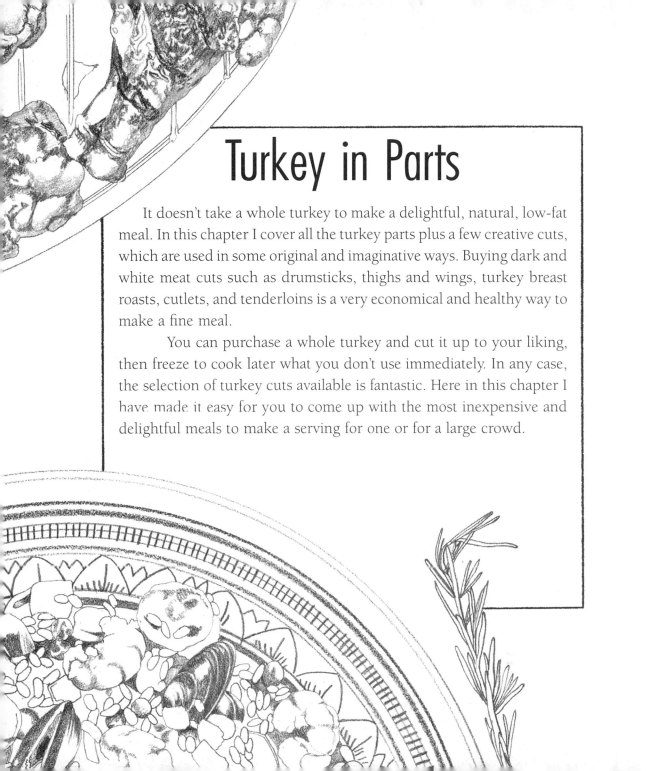

Turkey in Parts

It doesn't take a whole turkey to make a delightful, natural, low-fat meal. In this chapter I cover all the turkey parts plus a few creative cuts, which are used in some original and imaginative ways. Buying dark and white meat cuts such as drumsticks, thighs and wings, turkey breast roasts, cutlets, and tenderloins is a very economical and healthy way to make a fine meal.

You can purchase a whole turkey and cut it up to your liking, then freeze to cook later what you don't use immediately. In any case, the selection of turkey cuts available is fantastic. Here in this chapter I have made it easy for you to come up with the most inexpensive and delightful meals to make a serving for one or for a large crowd.

Fajitas with Lime-Vinegar Marinade

This is an easy and delicious meal that you bake instead of fry. The marinated turkey makes this a unique meal that only takes about 30 minutes to cook and is about 300 calories per serving. Serve with your favorite rice or beans.

Lime-Vinegar Marinade (see opposite)
1 pound turkey breast tenderloins
1 large onion, thinly sliced
1 large green bell pepper, sliced into thin strips
1 medium-size red bell pepper, sliced into thin strips
1 small jalapeño chile, minced (optional)
1 tablespoon vegetable oil
4 tortillas, warmed
Sour cream or guacamole and cilantro for topping

Lime wedges
Shredded lettuce

Lime-Vinegar Marinade

1/4 cup freshly squeezed lime juice (about 2 small limes)
1 tablespoon red wine vinegar
2 garlic cloves, crushed
1/2 teaspoon honey
1/4 teaspoon ground cumin
1/4 teaspoon ground coriander

Prepare marinade. Add the turkey, mix well, and refrigerate 1 hour or overnight, turning often.

Preheat oven to 400°F (205°C). Lightly oil a 15″ × 10″ baking pan. Combine onion, bell pepper, and chile, if using, in baking pan. Bake 10 minutes. Remove pan from the oven and push vegetables to one side of the pan. Remove turkey from the marinade and reserve the marinade for basting. Place turkey in pan, spread the partially cooked vegetables around the turkey, and add 2 tablespoons of the marinade. Bake 10 minutes, then baste with marinade and turn vegetables. Bake another 10 minutes or until the turkey is no longer pink in center when cut with a knife.

Thinly slice turkey and divide equally with the vegetables among warmed tortillas. Top with a little sour cream or guacamole and cilantro. Serve with lime wedges and lettuce. Makes 4 servings.

Lime-Vinegar Marinade
Mix together all of the ingredients for the marinade in a large plastic bag.

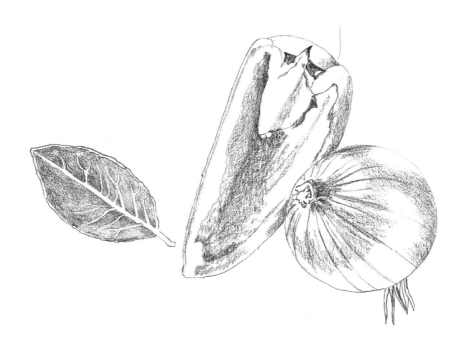

Turkey Cutlets with Champagne-Cream Sauce

This elegant entrée will please even the most finicky diner. Serve it with a rice pilaf,
a mixture of summer squash, and, of course, the rest of the champagne or a nice dry chardonnay.

1/4 cup all-purpose flour
1/2 teaspoon salt
1/8 teaspoon white pepper
1/4 teaspoon garlic powder
1/8 teaspoon dried tarragon
6 turkey breast cutlets

4 teaspoons butter
1/2 cup sliced shiitake mushrooms
1 tablespoon olive oil
1-1/2 cups champagne
1/4 cup half-and-half
2 tablespoons chopped parsley

Combine flour, salt, pepper, garlic powder, and tarragon in a large plastic bag. Place the turkey cutlets, one at a time, into the bag, and shake to coat with the flour mixture. Remove cutlets from bag and shake off any excess flour. Set aside leftover flour. Melt 1 teaspoon of the butter in a large skillet over medium heat. Add mushrooms and cook until softened. Remove with a slotted spoon and set aside.

Heat remaining butter and olive oil in same skillet and add turkey cutlets. Cook until browned on one side. Turn cutlets and pour in champagne. Simmer, uncovered, about 15 minutes or until the cutlets are no longer pink in center when cut with a knife. Remove the turkey from the pan and keep warm.

Increase heat to high. Reduce cooking juices by half. Whisk together the remaining flour and half-and-half and whisk into reduced cooking liquid. Cook, stirring, until thickened. Add reserved mushrooms to the sauce. Place turkey cutlets on warmed plates and spoon sauce over the cutlets. Garnish with parsley. Makes 4 to 6 servings.

Turkey Stroganoff

The classic beef Stroganoff, an American favorite, is made with turkey and nonfat sour cream for our health-conscious eaters. What a delicious way to enjoy eating without guilt.

1/4 cup all-purpose flour
1/2 teaspoon salt
1/8 teaspoon white pepper
2 pounds skinless boneless turkey breast, cut into
   1/4-inch slices
1/4 cup vegetable oil

1 medium-size white onion, finely chopped
1/2 pound brown mushrooms, sliced
1-1/2 cups Turkey Stock (page 2)
2 tablespoons port (optional)
1-1/4 cups nonfat sour cream

Combine flour, salt, and pepper in a large plastic bag. Add turkey slices and shake to coat with the flour mixture. Remove turkey from bag and shake off any excess flour.

Heat oil in a large skillet over medium-high heat. Add turkey and cook, stirring occasionally, until lightly browned. Remove turkey with a slotted spoon and drain on paper towels. Add onion to remaining oil in skillet and cook, stirring occasionally, until tender. Add mushrooms and cook over medium heat, stirring occasionally, 3 minutes.

Stir in stock and scrape up all browned bits. Add port, if using. Return turkey to skillet, cover, and simmer about 5 minutes. Stir in sour cream and simmer just enough to heat; do not boil or sauce will curdle. Serve over noodles or brown rice. Makes 4 servings.

Touch-of-the-Orient Turkey Cutlets with Apricots

The apricots, water chestnuts, and gingerroot make this a meal to remember.
The apricots just melt into the other ingredients. Serve over cooked rice.

1 tablespoon margarine
6 turkey breast cutlets
1 (10-ounce) jar apricot preserves
1/2 cup soy sauce
1 cup water
1 (8-ounce) can water chestnuts, drained and
   liquid reserved
10 to 12 dried apricots, coarsely chopped

1 tablespoon minced gingerroot
2 garlic cloves, crushed
3 celery stalks, sliced diagonally
2 cups sliced mushrooms
1 cup sliced green onions, including tops
3/4 cup green snow peas
1 large green bell pepper, sliced
Cooked rice

Melt margarine in a large skillet or wok over medium heat. Add turkey and brown on both sides. Stir in preserves, soy sauce, water, liquid from water chestnuts, dried apricots, gingerroot, and garlic. Simmer 40 minutes or until turkey is no longer pink in center when cut with a knife.

    Add celery, mushrooms, green onions, peas, bell pepper, and water chestnuts to skillet. Cook, stirring, 5 minutes, or until all ingredients are heated through. Serve over rice. Makes 4 servings.

Thai Turkey Curry

This curry contains coconut milk, jalapeños, and sweet basil, which give it a distinct Thai flavor. This curry is even better if cooked in advance and served the next day. Serve with my Hot Mango Chutney (page 100) on the side, if desired.

2 tablespoons vegetable oil
1 large onion, chopped
8 garlic cloves, chopped
4 jalapeño chiles, seeded and thinly sliced
1 tablespoon minced gingerroot
2 tablespoons fresh basil, chopped
2 tablespoons dried turmeric

2 tablespoons dried coriander
1 bay leaf
1-1/2 pounds turkey breast, cut into 1-inch cubes
3 cups coconut milk
2 chicken bouillon cubes
Cooked basmati rice

Heat oil in a large skillet over medium heat. Add onion, garlic, chiles, and gingerroot, and cook, stirring occasionally, until tender. Add basil, turmeric, coriander, bay leaf, and turkey. Increase heat to medium-high and cook, stirring occasionally, until turkey is browned, about 2 minutes. Add coconut milk and bouillon cubes. Reduce heat, cover, and simmer about 2 hours. Serve over rice. Makes 4 servings.

Note

Coconut milk is available canned in light and regular versions in ethnic markets and some supermarkets.

Stuffed Turkey Breast with Red-Pepper Stuffing

I serve this recipe when I entertain a group of ten to twelve. It is so easy to do and is absolutely delicious. When sliced and arranged on a platter, it looks so good people think you've been cooking all day. Serve it with your favorite steamed vegetables and some wild rice cooked with finely chopped pecans.

1 (4-pound) boneless turkey breast
1 (7-ounce) jar roasted red bell peppers
3-1/2 tablespoons margarine
1 large onion, chopped
3 garlic cloves, minced

3/4 teaspoon dried basil
Salt and freshly ground pepper to taste
1 cup whole-grain bread crumbs, toasted
1 tablespoon chopped parsley

Heat oven to 425°F (220°C). Remove tenderloins and reserve for another use. Lay turkey breast flat on a work surface, lightly pound meat to an even thickness with a meat mallet, and set aside. Drain peppers, pat dry, and set aside.

Melt 1 tablespoon of the margarine in a large skillet over medium heat. Add onion and cook 2 minutes or until softened. Add garlic and basil, and cook 1 minute. Remove from heat and add salt, pepper, bread crumbs, and parsley. Mix until blended and spread over pounded turkey breast. Cover with peppers. Roll up breast like a jellyroll, starting with a long side, and tie with string. Place in a roasting pan and rub with remaining margarine.

Place in oven, reduce oven temperature to 350°F (175°C), and roast turkey, basting occasionally with pan drippings, 2 hours or until meat thermometer registers 170°F (75°C) or until juices run clear when turkey is pierced with a skewer. Remove turkey from pan. Let stand 10 to 15 minutes before slicing. Makes 10 to 12 servings.

Turkey Cacciatore

This famous dish is just as good with turkey as with chicken—it is very flavorful and very Italian.

3 pounds boneless turkey cutlets, cut into 1-inch
   strips
1 cup all-purpose flour
1/4 cup each butter and olive oil
2 medium-size onions, chopped
3 garlic cloves, minced
1 (28-ounce) can Italian stewed tomatoes,
   drained and liquid reserved, chopped
1 large green bell pepper, thinly sliced
2 tablespoons chopped pimiento

2 tablespoons chopped Italian parsley
Salt to taste
1 tablespoon Italian seasoning
1/4 teaspoon white pepper
1 large bay leaf
1 cup dry red wine
2 cups thinly sliced mushrooms
Cooked pasta or rice

Preheat oven to 350°F (175°C). Pat turkey dry with paper towels. Pour flour into a large plastic bag. Add turkey strips and shake to coat lightly with flour. Remove turkey and shake to remove excess flour.

Heat butter and oil in a large Dutch oven over medium heat. Add turkey, a few pieces at a time, and cook until lightly browned, removing browned pieces to a warmed plate. Add onions and garlic to Dutch oven and cook until tender. Return turkey to Dutch oven and add remaining ingredients. Add 1/3 cup of reserved tomato liquid. Cover and bake 1 hour, adding 1/4 cup water if mixture becomes dry. Cook about another 1-1/2 hours or until turkey is tender. Serve over pasta or rice. Makes 8 to 10 servings.

Turkey Parmesan

A quick and easy way to make an Italian favorite that is sure to please your family.
It takes only about 30 minutes to prepare and is scrumptious to eat.

1 pound turkey breast cutlets, sliced 1/4 inch
   thick
2 (14-ounce) cans Italian stewed tomatoes
2 tablespoons cornstarch
1/2 tablespoon Italian seasoning

1/4 teaspoon hot pepper sauce (optional)
1/4 cup freshly grated Parmesan cheese
Chopped Italian parsley
Cooked rice or pasta

Preheat oven 425°F (220°C). Place turkey cutlets between two pieces of waxed paper or plastic wrap and pound with a meat mallet to slightly flatten. Place turkey in an 11″ × 7″ baking dish, cover, and bake 20 minutes or until turkey is no longer pink in center when cut with a knife.

Meanwhile, in a large saucepan over medium heat, combine tomatoes, cornstarch, Italian seasoning, and hot sauce. Cook, stirring, until thickened. Drain juices from baking dish, pour sauce over turkey, and top with cheese. Bake about 5 minutes or until cheese is melted. Garnish with parsley. Serve over pasta or rice. Makes 4 to 6 servings.

Paella with Turkey Sausage, Steamed Clams & Mu

A Spanish dish that you can now have right here at home. Serve steaming hot right fro

1 large onion, chopped
2 garlic cloves, minced
1 large green bell pepper, chopped
6 saffron strands dissolved in 1 tablespoon hot
   water
1 teaspoon salt
1 teaspoon paprika
1 pound spicy Italian-style turkey sausage, sliced
   1 inch thick

3 medium-size tomatoes, peeled and chopped
1-1/2 cups uncooked long-grain rice
3 cups Turkey Stock (page 2)
1 (10-ounce) package frozen green peas
1 (4-ounce) can diced pimientos, drained
1/2 pound firm-flesh fish fillets, cubed
1 pound raw shrimp, shelled and deveined
10 to 12 clams, in shells, well scrubbed
8 to 10 mussels, in shells, well scrubbed

Heat olive oil in a large Dutch oven. Add onion, garlic, and bell pepper, and cook until tender. Add saffron, salt, and paprika. Stir in sausage, tomatoes, rice, and stock. Cover and cook 30 minutes. Add peas, pimientos, fish, and shrimp. Cover pan and cook 15 minutes.

Meanwhile, in a large separate saucepan, cover clams and mussels with enough water and cook over medium heat 6 to 10 minutes, or until shells open. Discard any clams or mussels that do not open. Arrange clams and mussels in rice mixture so that they are covered with rice but you can still see their shells. Serve from the Dutch oven. Makes 8 to 10 servings.

Honey-grilled Turkey Tenderloins

Hot off the grill, with soy sauce, honey, a dash of sherry, and lots of garlic, it's a favorite come summertime when you have company and it's too hot to cook indoors. Serve with a mixed green salad and garlic bread.

1 pound turkey tenderloins
2 tablespoons soy sauce
2 tablespoons sherry
1 tablespoon honey

1 teaspoon sesame seeds
1/2 teaspoon sesame oil
2 garlic cloves, minced

Slice turkey tenderloins lengthwise, cutting almost through. Open halves flat. In a large bowl, combine soy sauce, sherry, honey, sesame seeds, sesame oil, and garlic. Place turkey tenderloins in mixture and turn to coat. Cover and marinate in refrigerator 1 hour.

Prepare grill for direct cooking. Drain tenderloins; discard marinade. Place tenderloins on grill and cover grill. Cook 6 minutes. Turn and grill 5 minutes or until turkey is no longer pink in center when cut with a knife. Makes 4 servings.

Thai Turkey Satay

Serve this as either an appetizer or a main dish.

1 pound turkey tenderloins
1/4 cup canned coconut milk
2 tablespoons minced white onion
1 teaspoon soy sauce
1/2 teaspoon crushed red pepper flakes
  (optional)
1/4 teaspoon ground ginger
1/2 teaspoon grated lime peel

Spicy Peanut Sauce

3 garlic cloves
1 cup smooth peanut butter
1/4 cup sugar
1/4 cup water
1/2 teaspoon Vietnamese garlic-chili paste, or
  to taste
1 tablespoon fresh lemon juice
1 tablespoon soy sauce

Cut turkey tenderloins in half lengthwise. Place between 2 pieces of waxed paper and pound lightly with a meat mallet to flatten evenly. Cut lengthwise into 1-inch strips. In a large plastic bag, combine coconut milk, onion, soy sauce, pepper flakes, ginger, and lime peel. Add turkey strips to marinade, and marinate in the refrigerator 4 hours or overnight.

Prepare peanut sauce. Prepare grill for direct cooking. Soak 8 to 10 bamboo skewers in water 15 minutes. Drain turkey and discard marinade. Weave turkey strips onto skewers. Place skewers on grill and cover grill. Cook 3 minutes. Turn and grill another 3 minutes or until turkey is no longer pink in center when cut with a knife. Serve with peanut sauce. Makes 4 main-dish servings or 8 appetizer servings.

Spicy Peanut Sauce

Chop garlic in a small food processor and add remaining ingredients. Process until smooth. Cover and refrigerate up to 3 to 5 days.

Simply Delicious Roasted Drumsticks

These drumsticks are just that, simple and delicious.
Serve with my Traditional English Roasties (page 95) and your favorite vegetable.

1 or more turkey drumstick/s

Preheat oven to 350°F (175°C). Place turkey on a rack in a large baking pan. Bake 45 minutes, baste, and turn turkey over. Bake another 45 minutes or until a meat thermometer registers 170°F (75°C) or until juices run clear when turkey is pierced with a skewer. Makes 2 servings for each leg.

 Note

Drumsticks are usually available in sizes ranging from 1/2 to 1-1/2 pounds. Occasionally larger drumsticks are available, and these are better for stuffing. Number of servings and cooking times will vary depending on the size of drumsticks available.

Stuffed Turkey Drumsticks

These turkey drumsticks are very moist and flavorful. Drumsticks are by far my favorite part of the turkey. When cooked, the meat should just fall off the bone. Serve with one of the cranberry relishes and a potato dish from the All the Trimmings chapter, and your favorite vegetable dish.

About 3/4 cup vegetable oil
1 medium-size onion, chopped
1/4 cup chopped mushrooms
1/2 pound lean ground turkey or chicken
1/4 teaspoon dried sage

1/2 teaspoon dried thyme
1/2 teaspoon fresh chopped parsley
Salt and pepper to taste
1/4 cup almonds, finely ground
4 large turkey drumsticks

Preheat oven to 350°F (175°C). Heat 1/4 cup of the oil in a medium-size skillet over medium heat. Add onion and mushrooms, and cook until tender. Add ground turkey and cook, stirring to break up turkey, until turkey is no longer pink. Add sage, 1/4 teaspoon of the thyme, chopped parsley, salt, and pepper. Stir almonds into ground turkey mixture. Let this mixture cool down before you stuff the drumsticks.

Rinse drumsticks and pat dry with paper towels. Pull skin all the way back to small end of each leg. With a sharp knife, make 4 slits in each leg 3-1/2 inches long and 1 inch deep.

Stuff each leg slit with the stuffing mixture, filling until full but not overflowing. Sprinkle stuffed drumsticks with remaining thyme and season with salt and pepper. Pour 1 teaspoon of the oil over each leg and then carefully pull skin back over drumsticks.

Place drumsticks on a rack in a large roasting pan. Pour 1 tablespoon oil over each leg and bake 1 hour. Turn drumsticks over and bake 45 minutes or until drumsticks are very tender. Makes 4 to 6 servings.

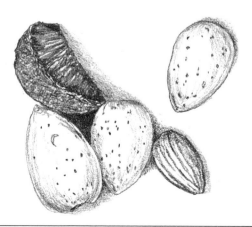

Salt-cured Roasted Drumsticks

These drumsticks are cured in salt overnight and slow-cooked in the oven. The onions add a rich, sweet flavor. Serve with a potato dish and your favorite steamed vegetable.

4 turkey drumsticks
3 tablespoons coarse salt
2 teaspoons dried thyme

6 tablespoons vegetable oil
2 medium-size onions, quartered
1/2 teaspoon white pepper

Rub each leg well with salt and thyme. Place legs in a dish; cover and refrigerate at least 12 hours.

Preheat oven to 325°F (165°C). Coat a large roasting pan with 1 tablespoon of the oil. Rinse salt off drumsticks and pat dry with paper towels. Arrange drumsticks in the prepared pan and pour 1-1/2 tablespoons of oil over drumsticks. Toss onions with remaining oil and the pepper. Scatter onions in pan around turkey and bake 1 hour. Turn turkey over and bake 45 minutes or until drumsticks are tender and onions are golden brown. Makes 4 servings.

Turkey Drumsticks Smothered in Roasted Garlic & Red Basil Gravy

This recipe has a Creole flavoring to it. The roasted garlic along with the sweet basil red gravy makes a rich flavor.

30 unpeeled garlic cloves
1 cup all-purpose flour
2 tablespoons Chef Paul Prudhomme's Poultry Magic
2 turkey drumsticks
2 cups olive oil
2 cups chopped onions
3 bay leaves

1 large green bell pepper, chopped
1 (28-ounce) can Creole-style stewed tomatoes
1 (8-ounce) can tomato sauce
1-1/2 teaspoons dried basil
2 tablespoons light brown sugar
4 cups Turkey Stock (page 2) or chicken broth
Salt to taste
Cooked pasta or rice

Preheat oven to 400°F (205°C). Arrange garlic cloves on a large baking sheet so they do not touch. Roast 12 to 15 minutes or until skins are dry looking and ends start to turn brown. Cool to room temperature, peel, and set aside. Reduce oven to 350°F (175°C).

Combine flour and Poultry Magic in a large plastic bag. Add drumsticks and shake to coat. Remove drumsticks and shake off excess flour. Reserve remaining flour mixture.

Heat oil in a Dutch oven over medium-high heat. Add drumsticks and cook, turning, until evenly browned. Drain drumsticks on paper towels. Pour off all but 1/4 cup of the oil from the pan.

Preheat pan over medium heat. Add onions, 1 tablespoon of the reserved flour mixture, and bay leaves, and cook until onions are tender, about 5 minutes. Add bell pepper and cook 2 minutes. Add tomatoes, increase heat to high and cook 1 minute. Stir in tomato sauce, basil, roasted garlic, and brown sugar. Cook about 5 minutes. Add 3-1/2 cups of stock. Return the browned turkey drumsticks to the Dutch oven and bring to a boil on top of stove.

Cover Dutch oven and bake 1 hour, adding remaining 1/2 cup stock as needed. Bake 30 minutes or until turkey is very tender and meat falls freely off bones. Remove bay leaves and discard. Serve turkey and gravy with cooked pasta or rice. Makes 4 servings.

Garlic Lover's Turkey Drumsticks

If you love garlic, then you'll love these turkey drumsticks, which are stuffed with fresh garlic and seasoned with garlic powder. Serve them with a cranberry relish and your favorite side dish from All the Trimmings chapter.

4 large turkey drumsticks
6 garlic cloves, thinly sliced
3 teaspoons garlic powder

Salt and freshly ground pepper to taste
8 tablespoons vegetable oil

Preheat oven to 350°F (175°C). Rinse turkey and pat dry with paper towels. Pull skin all the way back to the small end of each leg. With a sharp knife, make 4 slits in each leg 3-1/2 inches long and 1 inch deep. Stuff each slit with 3 to 4 garlic slices. Season drumsticks with garlic powder, salt, and pepper. Pour 1 tablespoon of the oil over each leg. Very carefully pull skin back over each leg and place drumsticks on a rack in a large baking pan. Season with pepper and pour 1 tablespoon of the oil over each leg.

Bake drumsticks 1 hour. Turn, baste with pan drippings, and bake 45 minutes or until drumsticks are tender. Makes 4 servings.

Braised Turkey Drumsticks

Turkey drumsticks simmer in white wine, turkey stock, garlic, onion, and thyme for 2 hours to make one of the most delicious meals ever—with moist tender meat and yummy gravy— a meal to remember.

1/4 cup margarine
4 turkey drumsticks
3 garlic cloves, minced
1 cup diagonally sliced celery
1-1/2 cups diagonally sliced carrots
1 large onion, sliced and separated into rings
1/2 cup sliced mushrooms

1/2 cup Turkey Stock (page 2) or chicken broth
1/2 cup white wine
1 teaspoon salt
1/8 teaspoon freshly ground pepper
1 tablespoon all-purpose flour
2 tablespoons water

Melt margarine in a large Dutch oven over medium heat. Add turkey and cook, turning, until evenly browned. Remove turkey and set aside. Add garlic, celery, carrots, onion, and mushrooms to Dutch oven and cook, stirring occasionally, until onion is soft, about 3 minutes. Stir in stock, wine, salt, and pepper. Bring to a boil.

Return turkey to pan. Reduce heat, cover, and simmer about 1-1/2 hours or until the drumsticks are very tender and meat comes away from bone very easily. With a slotted spoon, transfer turkey and vegetables to a warmed platter; keep warm.

In a small bowl, combine flour and water to make a smooth paste. Over high heat, quickly reduce liquid in Dutch oven to about 1/3 cup. Blend in the flour mixture and cook, stirring constantly, until thickened. Pour sauce over the turkey and vegetables. Serve immediately. Makes 4 servings.

Curried Turkey Drumsticks

These drumsticks are very spicy; you may want to tame them down a bit. But if you like your curry spicy and the true taste of Bombay, this curry is the one you want. Serve with cooked basmati rice and my mango chutney along with your favorite vegetable and Indian condiments.

1 (12-ounce) bottle Scottish ale
1 (12-ounce) bottle Guinness stout
2 cups water
3 chicken bouillon cubes
4 garlic cloves, minced
3 teaspoons curry powder
1/4 cup Patak's Original Rogan Josh curry paste
   (found in specialty shops) or other curry paste
1-1/2 teaspoons garam masala

1 pinch hot red pepper flakes
1 pinch saffron
1 teaspoon dried tarragon
1/4 cup vegetable oil
2 large red onions, chopped
2/3 cup chopped mushrooms
2 turkey drumsticks
Cooked basmati rice
Hot Mango Chutney (page 100)

In a large Dutch oven, combine ale, stout, water, bouillon cubes, garlic, curry powder, curry paste, garam masala, pepper flakes, saffron, and tarragon. Bring to a boil, reduce heat, and simmer 1 hour.

In a large skillet, heat oil over medium heat. Add onions and cook until softened. Add mushrooms and cook until softened. Remove onions and mushrooms with a slotted spoon, and add to the curry mixture. Add turkey to skillet and cook, turning, until lightly browned. Add turkey to the curry mixture and cover turkey with onions, mushrooms, and sauce.

Cook about 1-1/2 hours, turning turkey over occasionally and spooning the onions, mushrooms, and sauce over the top of turkey. The meat should fall off the bone quite easily when pierced with a fork. Serve over rice with mango chutney. Makes 2 to 3 servings.

Spicy Barbecued Drumsticks

*These are great when you have a party. Their easy preparation and fabulous taste
are sure to please everyone. Cook as many as your grill will hold.*

4 to 6 turkey drumsticks
2 to 3 teaspoons garlic powder
Freshly ground pepper

Favorite Barbecue Sauce (page 98), Pineapple-
  Ginger Sauce (page 99), or barbecue sauce
  of your choice

Prepare grill for direct cooking using mesquite charcoal. Rinse turkey and pat dry with paper towels. When coals are ready, add a handful of hickory chips.

Arrange turkey on grill rack, cover grill, and cook 30 minutes. Baste with sauce and cook 30 minutes. Baste with sauce again and turn turkey over. Cook 30 minutes, baste, and at this point check to see if turkey is tender by testing with a fork. If turkey is not tender, keep checking every 15 to 30 minutes. Serve one drumstick per person. Makes 4 to 6 servings.

Pot-roasted Turkey Drumsticks

Pot roast takes on a whole new meaning when it's turkey in the pot. These drumsticks are cooked in a Dutch oven with seasoned stock, potatoes, onions, carrots, mushrooms, and also cabbage.

3-1/2 cups Turkey Stock (page 2) or chicken
   broth
1 teaspoon garlic powder
1 teaspoon Italian seasoning
1/2 teaspoon dried sage
Salt and freshly ground pepper to taste
2 garlic cloves, thinly sliced

1 large onion, chopped
2 large carrots, cut into pieces
1 cup thinly sliced mushrooms
1 small cabbage, cut into quarters
4 turkey drumsticks, rinsed and patted dry with
   paper towels

Preheat oven to 350°F (175°C). Combine stock, garlic powder, Italian seasoning, sage, salt, pepper, garlic, onion, carrots, mushrooms, and cabbage in a large Dutch oven and simmer 30 minutes.

Add turkey, cover, and bake 2 hours, or until drumsticks are tender when tested with a fork. Remove turkey with a slotted spoon and place on a warmed platter. Remove vegetables with a slotted spoon and place in a warm bowl. Pour cooking juices into a gravy boat and serve with turkey and vegetables. Makes 4 servings.

Mesquite-smoked Turkey Thighs

These smoky-flavored turkey thighs are basted with ginger, honey, and butter near the end of the cooking time. Serve with corn on the cob and salad of your choice.

2 (1-1/2-pound) turkey thighs
Salt and freshly ground pepper to taste
2 tablespoons olive oil

6 tablespoons butter
1 teaspoon honey
1 teaspoon ground ginger

Prepare grill for indirect cooking. When coals are ready, add a handful of mesquite or hickory chips.

Lift the skin away from meat and sprinkle meat with salt and pepper. Pull the skin back over meat and rub skin with oil.

In a small pan, melt butter. Stir in honey and ginger until blended. Set aside.

Arrange turkey on grill rack and cover grill. Cook, turning occasionally, about 1-1/2 hours or until golden brown. Brush turkey with ginger mixture about 10 minutes before the end of cooking. Transfer to a carving board, drizzle remaining ginger mixture over turkey, and cut into slices. Makes 3 or 4 servings.

Roasted Turkey Thigh Sandwiches

Sliced warm roasted turkey thighs placed on toasted whole-wheat bread with mayonnaise, mustard, lettuce, tomato, and red onion make easy turkey sandwiches that the whole family will enjoy.

2 turkey thighs, about 1 pound each
Salt and freshly ground pepper to taste
8 slices whole-wheat bread
4 lettuce leaves

2 medium-size tomatoes, thinly sliced
4 slices red onion
1/4 cup mayonnaise
1/4 cup mustard

Preheat oven to 350°F (175°C). Place turkey on a rack in a medium-size baking pan. Bake 30 minutes, turn over, and bake another 10 to 15 minutes or until juices run clear when pierced with a fork.

Cool about 10 minutes. Place turkey on a cutting board. Slice turkey into thin slices and place on a plate. Arrange bread, lettuce, tomatoes, and red onion on separate plates or on one large plate. Let each person make his or her own sandwich, adding mayonnaise and mustard as desired. Makes 4 servings.

Spicy Hickory-smoked Turkey Wings in Beer Sauce

The secret to this dish is to simmer the turkey wings in the beer before you grill them. Grilling adds their hickory-smoked flavor and the spicy sauce makes these a dish that everyone will want to make again.

3 (12-ounce) cans of domestic light beer
Salt and freshly ground pepper to taste
4 large turkey wings
1 (14-ounce) can Mexican-style stewed
    tomatoes, drained
1/2 cup chopped onion

1/2 cup cider vinegar
1/3 cup butter or margarine, melted
2 tablespoons light brown sugar
2 tablespoons Worcestershire sauce
1 teaspoon chili powder

In a large saucepan, bring beer, salt, and pepper to a boil. Add turkey wings. Reduce heat, cover, and simmer wings 30 minutes. Remove wings and set aside. Reserve 1/2 cup of the cooking liquid.

Add tomatoes, onion, vinegar, 1/2 cup beer broth, butter, brown sugar, Worcestershire sauce, and chili powder to a blender. Blend until smooth. Pour tomato mixture into a large saucepan. Simmer 20 minutes or until slightly thickened. Reserve half of the sauce for basting and the other half to accompany grilled wings.

Prepare grill for direct cooking, adding some soaked hickory chips. Place wings on rack and cover grill. Cook, basting frequently with the reserved turkey beer broth mixture, about 30 minutes or until browned and juices run clear when pierced with a fork. Serve wings with remaining sauce. Makes 4 servings.

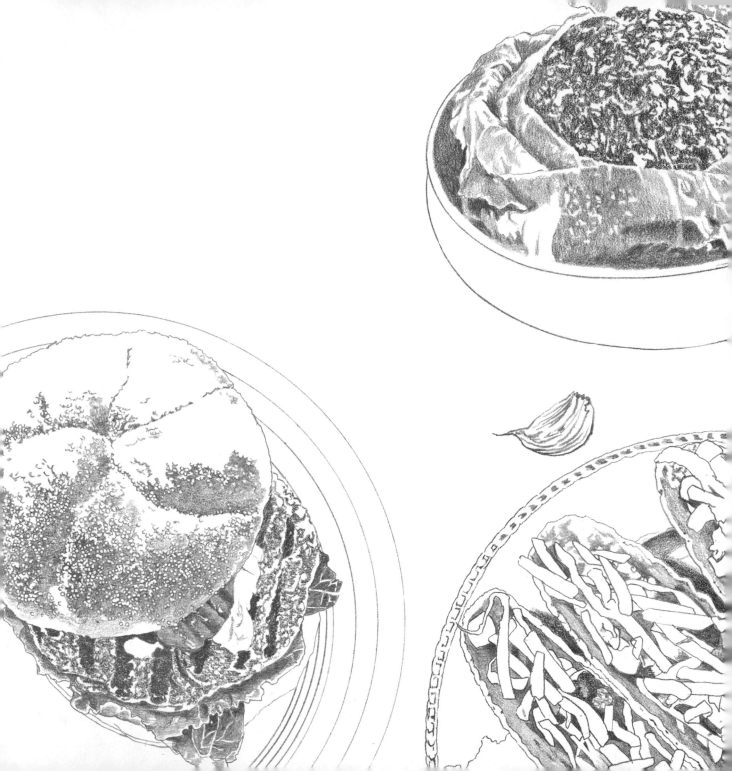

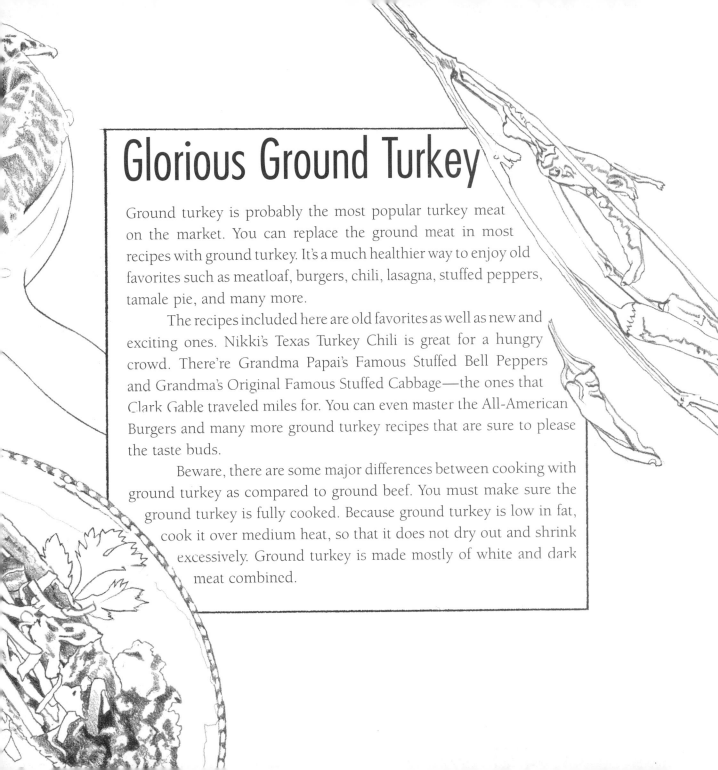

Glorious Ground Turkey

Ground turkey is probably the most popular turkey meat on the market. You can replace the ground meat in most recipes with ground turkey. It's a much healthier way to enjoy old favorites such as meatloaf, burgers, chili, lasagna, stuffed peppers, tamale pie, and many more.

The recipes included here are old favorites as well as new and exciting ones. Nikki's Texas Turkey Chili is great for a hungry crowd. There're Grandma Papai's Famous Stuffed Bell Peppers and Grandma's Original Famous Stuffed Cabbage—the ones that Clark Gable traveled miles for. You can even master the All-American Burgers and many more ground turkey recipes that are sure to please the taste buds.

Beware, there are some major differences between cooking with ground turkey as compared to ground beef. You must make sure the ground turkey is fully cooked. Because ground turkey is low in fat, cook it over medium heat, so that it does not dry out and shrink excessively. Ground turkey is made mostly of white and dark meat combined.

All-American Burgers

I cook these on my outdoor grill, and I have even fooled some people into thinking that they are actually beef. Indulge and enjoy.

1 pound extra-lean ground turkey
2 tablespoons dried bread crumbs
1/2 cup chopped onion
2 teaspoons Worcestershire sauce
1/4 cup ketchup
2 garlic cloves, minced

1 teaspoon coarsely cracked pepper
4 whole-wheat hamburger buns
1/4 cup mayonnaise
4 lettuce leaves
4 slices red onion
4 slices tomato

Prepare charcoal grill for direct cooking. Combine turkey, bread crumbs, onion, Worcestershire sauce, ketchup, garlic, and pepper in a medium-size bowl. Shape into 4 round patties, about 3-1/2 inches in diameter. Place burgers on grill rack and cover grill. Cook 5 minutes on each side or until no longer pink in center when tested with a knife. Burgers must be fully cooked.

Serve immediately on buns with mayonnaise, lettuce, onion, and tomato. Makes 4 servings.

Bacon & Mushroom Cheeseburgers

These turkey burgers are baked, not grilled.

1 pound lean ground turkey
2 tablespoons dried bread crumbs
1/2 (10-3/4-ounce) can condensed cream of
  mushroom soup
2 eggs, slightly beaten
1 small onion, finely chopped
1/2 cup chopped mushrooms
1 tablespoon freshly ground Parmesan cheese
1/4 teaspoon freshly ground pepper
1/2 teaspoon salt, or to taste

1/4 teaspoon dried oregano
4 slices Monterey Jack or Cheddar cheese
4 whole-wheat hamburger buns
1/4 cup mayonnaise
1/4 cup mustard (optional)
4 lettuce leaves
4 thin slices red onion
4 slices ripe tomato
8 slices bacon, cooked

Preheat oven to 350°F (175°C). In a large bowl, combine turkey, bread crumbs, mushroom soup, eggs, onion, mushrooms, Parmesan, pepper, salt, and oregano, and mix well. Shape into 4 round patties, about 3-1/2 inches in diameter. Place in a baking pan large enough to hold all 4 patties.

Bake 30 minutes and turn. Bake 15 minutes or until no longer pink in center when tested with a knife. Burgers must be fully cooked. Top each burger with 1 slice of cheese and bake until cheese melts, about 1 minute.

Serve immediately on buns with mayonnaise, mustard, if using, lettuce, onion, tomato, and bacon. Makes 4 servings.

Mushroom Turkey Loaf with Mashed Potato Topping

I love this meal because it's quick, easy to make, and wonderful to eat.

1 pound lean ground turkey
1/2 cup dried bread crumbs
2 egg whites
1/4 cup finely chopped onion
1/4 cup chopped mushrooms

2 teaspoons Worcestershire sauce
1/2 teaspoon salt, or to taste
1/2 cup condensed cream of mushroom soup
2 medium-size russet potatoes, peeled, cooked, and mashed

Preheat oven to 350°F (175°C). In a large bowl, combine turkey, bread crumbs, egg whites, onion, mushrooms, Worcestershire sauce, salt, and 1/4 cup mushroom soup, and mix well. Shape loaf in a 2-quart baking dish. Score loaf by making several diagonal grooves across top with a table knife. Fill grooves with remaining 1/4 cup mushroom soup.

Bake 40 minutes or until center of loaf reads 170°F (75°C) on an instant-read thermometer and juices run clear when loaf is pierced with a skewer. Remove the loaf from the oven. With a spatula, spread the mashed potatoes evenly on top of loaf. Bake another 10 minutes or until top of potato mixture is a light golden brown. Makes 6 servings.

Little Turkey Loaves

Enjoy these at lunch with a salad on the side or take them to a party as an appetizer. Whichever way they're served, you'll enjoy them. Kids also love these tiny loaves.

1 pound lean ground turkey
1 small apple, peeled, cored, and chopped
1/2 small onion, chopped
1/2 cup rolled oats
2 teaspoons Dijon mustard

1 teaspoon dried rosemary
1/2 teaspoon salt, or to taste
Freshly ground pepper to taste
Cranberry sauce

Preheat oven to 400°F (205°C). Grease 12 muffin cups. In a large bowl, combine turkey, apple, onion, oats, mustard, rosemary, salt, and pepper, and mix well. Press mixture into muffin cups.

Bake 20 minutes or until lightly browned and centers are no longer pink. Remove from cups and place on a platter. Top each loaf with a small spoonful of cranberry sauce. Makes 4 servings.

Luscious Turkey Lasagna

I usually serve this dish after a football game. Serve with a tossed green salad
and garlic bread for a winning combination.

2 tablespoons olive oil
2 medium-size onions, minced
2 garlic cloves, crushed
1 pound lean ground turkey
1/2 cup sliced mushrooms
1-1/2 teaspoons salt, or to taste
1/4 teaspoon freshly ground pepper
1/2 teaspoon dried oregano
3 tablespoons chopped fresh parsley

1 (28-ounce) can Italian-style tomatoes in puree
1 (8-ounce) can tomato paste
1/2 cup freshly grated Parmesan cheese
1/2 pound lasagna noodles
1 (10-ounce) package frozen spinach, thawed and drained
1 pound (4 cups) shredded mozzarella cheese
1 pound ricotta cheese or cottage cheese

In a medium-size skillet, heat oil over medium heat. Add onions and garlic, and cook until lightly browned. Add turkey and cook, stirring to break up meat, until no longer pink. Blend in mushrooms, salt, pepper, oregano, parsley, tomatoes, tomato paste, and 2 tablespoons of the Parmesan cheese. Simmer 45 minutes.

Preheat oven to 350°F (175°C). Cook noodles in boiling salted water according to package directions until just tender. Drain and cover with cold water. Arrange one-third of the meat sauce in a 13" × 9" baking dish. Cover with a layer of lasagna noodles, then a layer of half the spinach, then a layer of half the mozzarella cheese, then a layer of half the ricotta cheese. Sprinkle with 2 tablespoons of the Parmesan cheese. Repeat layers, ending with a layer of sauce and remaining Parmesan cheese.

Bake about 1 hour or until bubbly and heated through. Let stand 10 minutes before serving. Makes 6 to 8 servings.

Variation

To make ahead, assemble lasagna, cover, and refrigerate overnight. Bake in preheated oven just before serving.

Nikki's Texas Turkey Chili

This chili is great! I heard about it through our friends, country music stars Jessi and Waylon Jennings, so I asked their assistant, Nikki, if she would send me her recipe. It's now one of our favorite turkey meals. The longer it simmers, the better, and the next day it's even better, if there is any left.

1 tablespoon vegetable oil
3 pounds lean ground turkey
1 (8-ounce) can tomato sauce
2 cups water
2 (10-ounce) cans tomatoes and green chiles
5 tablespoons chili powder
2 tablespoons dried onion flakes
2 tablespoons garlic powder

1 teaspoon red (cayenne) pepper, or to taste
1 teaspoon salt, or to taste
2 tablespoons paprika
2 tablespoons dried oregano
1 (15-ounce) can pinto beans (optional), drained
Chopped red onions
Shredded Cheddar cheese

Heat oil in a Dutch oven over medium heat. Add turkey and cook, stirring to break up meat, until no longer pink. Drain off fat.

Add tomato sauce, water, tomatoes and chiles, chili powder, dried onion, garlic powder, cayenne, salt, paprika, and oregano to turkey. Cover and simmer 1 hour. Beans can be added during the last 15 minutes of cooking or heated separately and served on the side. Serve with onions and cheese. Makes 8 servings.

Variation

Recipe can be doubled.

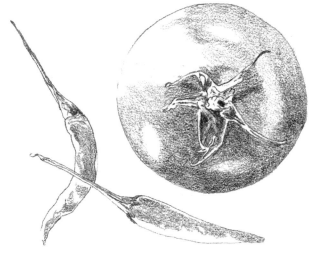

Grandma Papai's Famous Stuffed Bell Peppers

Grandma and Grandpa Papai were born in Hungary. They moved to the United States in the early 1940s and lived in New York, where they became part-time cooks for Hungarian restaurants. They later moved to California and opened their own restaurant, with a menu that featured half American and half Hungarian food. People would go across town to have these stuffed peppers—Clark Gable loved them—and my grandmother's other specialty, stuffed cabbage rolls (page 46). My grandmother could cook anything and make magic in the kitchen. Now you can have these two wonderful recipes in your own home.

6 large green bell peppers
Salt
2 tablespoons butter
1 medium-size onion, chopped
1 pound ground turkey
Freshly ground pepper to taste
1/2 teaspoon paprika

1 (16-ounce) can tomatoes, chopped and
    drained
1/2 cup water
1/2 cup uncooked white rice
1 egg
1 teaspoon Worcestershire sauce (optional)
2 cups Turkey Stock (page 2) or chicken broth

Cut the tops off the bell peppers; remove seeds and membrane. Precook bell peppers in boiling salted water about 5 minutes. For crisper stuffed peppers, omit precooking. Drain peppers and sprinkle a little salt inside each pepper.

Melt butter in a large skillet over medium heat. Add onion and cook until transparent. Add turkey and cook, stirring to break up meat, until no longer pink. Add salt, pepper, paprika, tomatoes, water, rice, egg, and Worcestershire sauce, and mix well. Reduce heat to low; cover and simmer until rice is tender, about 15 minutes.

Preheat oven to 350°F (175°C). Stuff bell peppers with rice mixture; stand upright in a baking dish just big enough to hold stuffed peppers. Add stock to dish.

Bake 30 minutes or until the tops are crusty and brown. Arrange stuffed peppers in a serving dish and gently pour cooking juices over stuffed peppers. Makes 6 servings.

Grandma's Original Famous Stuffed Cabbage

If I had to choose my favorite dish that Grandma made, it's probably this one.
She would sometimes cook this dish, refrigerate it overnight, and serve it the next day.

3 tablespoons uncooked rice
5 tablespoons water
1 (1-1/2-pound) green cabbage
4 slices bacon
1 large onion, chopped
2 pounds lean beef short ribs
2 teaspoons Hungarian paprika
1 tomato, sliced

1 medium-size green bell pepper, chopped
2 pounds sauerkraut, rinsed and drained
1 potato, peeled and grated
1 apple, peeled, cored, and grated
2 bay leaves
1-1/2 pounds lean ground turkey
1 egg
Salt and freshly ground pepper to taste

In a small saucepan, simmer rice and water, covered, 10 minutes or until tender. Bring a large pot of water to a boil. Add cabbage and cook 5 minutes. Remove cabbage and drain. Cool 5 to 10 minutes and remove leaves, one by one, very carefully. Trim off the thick heavy ribs.

Brown bacon in a 3-quart Dutch oven over medium heat. Remove bacon and set aside. Add onion to bacon drippings and cook until transparent.

Transfer half of cooked onion to a large bowl and set aside. Add short ribs and cooked bacon to onion in Dutch oven. Add enough water to cover and simmer, covered, 30 minutes. Increase heat to medium. Add paprika, tomato, bell pepper, sauerkraut, potato, apple, and bay leaves. Cook, covered, 20 minutes or until the sauerkraut begins to simmer.

Meanwhile, make cabbage rolls. Add turkey, egg, cooked rice, salt, and pepper to onion in bowl and mix well. Place a large tablespoon of turkey mixture on each cabbage leaf. Roll up, tucking edges in as you roll.

Add cabbage rolls to Dutch oven and bring to a boil. Reduce heat; cover and simmer 1-1/2 hours. Remove bay leaves and discard. Remove cabbage rolls from pan and set aside. Spoon a helping of sauerkraut mixture on each plate and top with 1 to 2 short ribs, 1 to 2 cabbage rolls, and a bacon slice. Spoon cooking juices over each serving. Makes 6 or 7 servings.

Tiburon Tamale Pie

A classic Mexican dish, it's like having chili with a cornmeal crust,
only made with turkey instead of beef.

2 tablespoons vegetable oil
1 cup chopped onion
1 cup chopped green pepper
1 pound ground turkey
2 (8-ounce) cans tomato sauce
1 (12-ounce) can whole-kernel corn, drained
1 cup pitted ripe olives, sliced
2 garlic cloves, minced
1 tablespoon light brown sugar

1-1/2 teaspoons salt
1 teaspoon ground cumin
1/2 tablespoon paprika
2 to 3 teaspoons chili powder
Freshly ground pepper
3/4 cup (3 ounces) shredded Cheddar cheese
3/4 cup yellow cornmeal
2 cups cold water
1 tablespoon butter

Heat oil in a large skillet over medium heat. Add onion and bell pepper, and cook until tender. Add turkey and cook, stirring to break up meat, until no longer pink. Stir in tomato sauce, corn, olives, garlic, sugar, 1 teaspoon of the salt, cumin, paprika, chili powder, and pepper. Simmer 20 to 25 minutes or until mixture is thick. Add 1/2 cup of the cheese. Stir until cheese melts.

Preheat oven to 375°F (190°C). Grease a 9-inch-square baking dish. Spoon turkey mixture into baking dish.

In a medium-size saucepan, stir cornmeal and remaining 1/2 teaspoon salt into cold water. Cook over medium heat, stirring constantly, about 10 minutes or until thickened. Stir in butter. Spoon over turkey mixture.

Bake about 30 minutes. Sprinkle with remaining cheese and bake another 10 minutes or until cheese melts. Makes 6 servings.

Easy Turkey Chili con Carne

This is another classic Mexican dish that is very tasty and very easy to make.

2 tablespoons vegetable oil
1 cup chopped onion
3/4 cup chopped green bell pepper
2 garlic cloves, minced
1 pound lean ground turkey
2 (8-ounce) cans Mexican-style stewed tomatoes,
   drained and crushed

2 cups cooked or canned red kidney beans
1 (8-ounce) can tomato sauce
Salt and freshly ground pepper to taste
2 teaspoons chili powder
1 bay leaf

Heat oil in a large skillet over medium heat. Add onion, bell pepper, and garlic, and cook until vegetables are tender. Add turkey and cook, stirring to break up meat, until no longer pink. Stir in tomatoes, beans, tomato sauce, salt, pepper, chili powder, and bay leaf. Cover and simmer, stirring occasionally, 1 hour. Remove bay leaf and discard. Serve hot. Makes 4 servings.

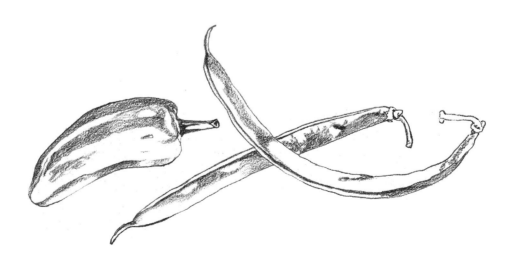

Soft Turkey Tacos

This is great when a small herd of big or little very hungry people turn up at your house, because it goes together quickly.

1-1/2 tablespoons vegetable oil
1 small onion, chopped
1 pound ground turkey
1 teaspoon dried oregano
Salt and freshly ground pepper to taste
1-1/2 tablespoons chili powder
1 (8-ounce) can tomato sauce
8 (6-inch) corn tortillas or 8 (10-inch) flour
   tortillas, warmed

1 small head iceberg lettuce, shredded
2 medium-size tomatoes, chopped
1 cup (4 ounces) shredded Cheddar cheese
Salsa
1 medium-size avocado (optional), peeled,
   pitted, and sliced
Dash of hot pepper sauce (optional)

Heat oil in a large skillet over medium heat. Add onion and cook until tender. Add turkey and cook, stirring to break up meat, until no longer pink. Mix in oregano, salt, pepper, and chili powder. Stir in tomato sauce. Bring to a boil, reduce heat, and simmer about 10 minutes or until turkey mixture is thickened. Keep warm.

Fill each tortilla with some turkey mixture. Top with lettuce, tomatoes, cheese, salsa and avocado and hot sauce, if using. Makes 4 to 8 servings.

Easy Turkey Goulash

I used to make this for my mom when I was a teenager and determined to impress her with my cooking. After spending the weekend with my grandmother and cooking meals together, I'd go home and try them on my mother. I now make this with turkey, instead of beef, and it's still my favorite quick meal.

2 tablespoons vegetable oil
1 large onion, chopped
2 garlic cloves, chopped
2 pounds lean ground turkey
1/4 cup all-purpose flour
1 tablespoon paprika
1 teaspoon salt, or to taste

1 teaspoon freshly ground pepper
1/4 teaspoon dried thyme
2 bay leaves
1 (14-ounce) can diced tomatoes
1 cup sour cream
Buttered noodles

Heat oil in a large skillet over medium heat. Add onion and garlic, and cook until onion is tender. Add turkey and cook, stirring to break up meat, until no longer pink. Stir in flour, paprika, salt, pepper, and thyme. Add bay leaves and tomatoes, cover, and simmer, stirring occasionally, until turkey is tender and mixture is thickened, about 1 hour. Remove bay leaves and discard. Stir in sour cream and heat through; do not boil. Serve hot, right out of skillet, over noodles. Makes 8 servings.

Bow-Ties with Italian Red Sauce

This meal is easy and quick, and like so many Italian dishes, the sauce is even better the next day.

1 pound ground turkey
Salt and freshly ground pepper to taste
1 teaspoon dried sage
1/8 teaspoon hot red pepper flakes
1 small onion, grated
1/4 cup olive oil
3 garlic cloves
1 (6-ounce) jar roasted red peppers, drained
   and chopped

1 (28-ounce) can Italian-style tomatoes in puree
1/2 cup chopped parsley
2 teaspoons dried Italian seasoning
1/2 teaspoon salt
1 pound bow-tie pasta, cooked and drained
Freshly grated Parmesan cheese

Place turkey in a medium-size bowl. Add salt, pepper, sage, pepper flakes and onion and mix well. Heat oil and garlic in a large heavy skillet over medium heat. Add turkey mixture and cook, stirring to break up meat, until turkey is no longer pink.

Add roasted peppers, tomatoes, parsley, Italian seasoning, and salt. Bring to a boil. Reduce heat, cover, and simmer 1 hour.

Toss sauce with pasta in a large bowl or serve pasta on individual warmed plates topped with a generous amount of sauce. Top with Parmesan cheese to taste. Makes 4 to 6 servings.

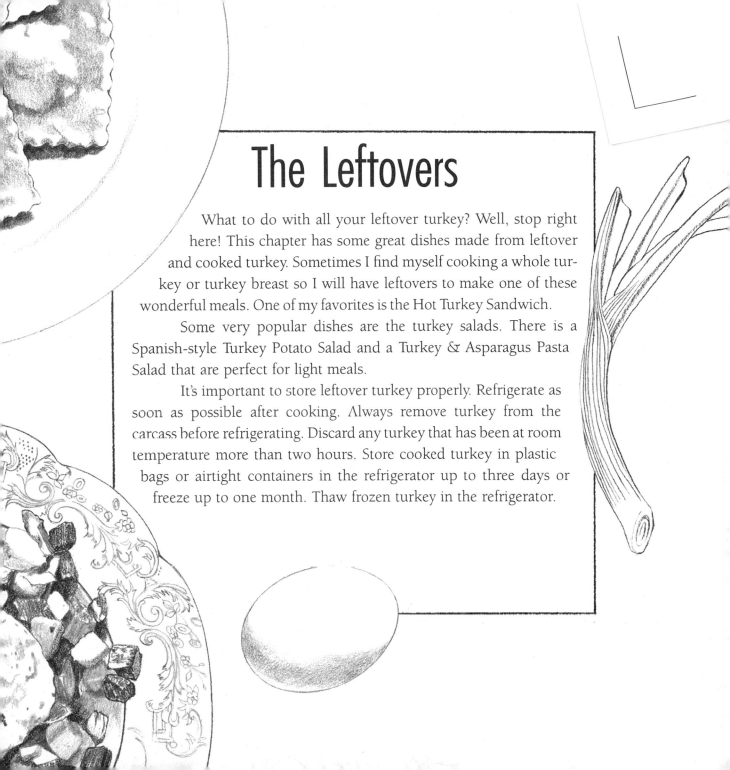

The Leftovers

What to do with all your leftover turkey? Well, stop right here! This chapter has some great dishes made from leftover and cooked turkey. Sometimes I find myself cooking a whole turkey or turkey breast so I will have leftovers to make one of these wonderful meals. One of my favorites is the Hot Turkey Sandwich.

Some very popular dishes are the turkey salads. There is a Spanish-style Turkey Potato Salad and a Turkey & Asparagus Pasta Salad that are perfect for light meals.

It's important to store leftover turkey properly. Refrigerate as soon as possible after cooking. Always remove turkey from the carcass before refrigerating. Discard any turkey that has been at room temperature more than two hours. Store cooked turkey in plastic bags or airtight containers in the refrigerator up to three days or freeze up to one month. Thaw frozen turkey in the refrigerator.

Turkey Tetrazzini

Invented at the Palace Hotel in San Francisco, this dish was originally made with chicken.
Over the years many cooks have changed it. Here is my version of this classic recipe.
Serve with garlic bread and steamed summer squash or a tossed green salad.

1/4 cup butter or margarine
1 green bell pepper, thinly sliced
1 cup sliced mushrooms
3 tablespoons all-purpose flour
1-1/2 teaspoons salt, or to taste
1/4 teaspoon white pepper
2-1/2 cups half-and-half

4 cups diced cooked turkey
1/4 cup sherry
1/4 teaspoon hot pepper sauce
6 ounces uncooked spaghetti
2 egg yolks, lightly beaten
Freshly grated Parmesan cheese

Preheat oven to 375°F (190°C). In a large skillet, melt butter over medium heat. Add bell pepper and 3/4 cup of the mushrooms, and cook until peppers are tender, about 5 minutes. Blend in flour, salt, and pepper. Stir in half-and-half and cook, stirring constantly, until thickened. Add turkey and sherry, and heat. Season with hot pepper sauce.

Meanwhile, cook spaghetti according to package directions. Drain spaghetti and turn into a large shallow casserole dish or 6 to 8 individual casserole dishes.

Add a small amount of the turkey mixture to egg yolks, then stir egg yolks into remaining turkey mixture. Spoon the sauce evenly over the spaghetti. Top with remaining mushroom slices and Parmesan cheese. Bake about 15 minutes for a large casserole or 8 minutes for individual ones, or until bubbly. Makes 6 to 8 servings.

Jambalaya

Perfect for a party, this dish serves twelve and because everything
is practically cooked already, it's easy to prepare.

3 cups uncooked rice, cooked
1/2 teaspoon saffron
1 cup cubed cooked ham
3 cups cubed or shredded cooked turkey
4 cups Turkey Stock (page 2) or chicken broth

36 oysters, shucked and liquor reserved
Clam broth
6 ounces cooked shelled shrimp
Salt and freshly ground pepper to taste

In a 4-quart saucepan, combine rice, saffron, ham, turkey, and stock. Simmer about 15 minutes to blend flavors.

In a large skillet, combine oysters and reserved liquor with enough clam broth to make 2 cups and cook over medium heat 3 minutes or until the edges of the oysters begin to curl. Add shrimp and oyster mixture to remaining ingredients and serve hot. Makes 12 servings.

All-in-One Turkey Dinner

Here is an economical way to feed your family the day after a fabulous turkey dinner with leftover turkey. Top this with homemade biscuits.

2 cups Turkey Stock (page 2) or chicken broth
1/2 pound small white boiling onions
6 medium-size carrots, peeled and cut into
   2-inch pieces
1 (10-ounce) package frozen lima beans
1/2 cup butter or margarine
1/2 cup all-purpose flour
1 teaspoon salt
1/8 teaspoon freshly ground pepper

1 teaspoon dried oregano
1 teaspoon Worcestershire sauce
2 cups milk
3 cups cubed cooked turkey

Biscuit Topping (optional)

2 cups biscuit mix
2/3 cup milk

Pour stock into a large kettle and bring to a boil. Add onions, carrots, and lima beans. Return to a boil. Reduce heat, cover, and simmer about 15 minutes or until vegetables are tender. Drain vegetables, reserving cooking liquid, and set vegetables aside.

Melt butter in a large saucepan. Remove from heat and stir in flour, salt, pepper, oregano, and Worcestershire sauce. Blend reserved cooking liquid into flour mixture and stir in the milk. Cook over medium heat, stirring constantly, until mixture thickens. Remove from heat. Stir in the turkey and cooked vegetables and keep warm while you make the biscuits, if using. Reheat turkey mixture if needed. Pour turkey mixture into a large, warmed dish and top with hot biscuits. Serve at once. Makes 6 servings.

Biscuit Topping

Preheat oven to 450°F (230°C). Grease a baking sheet. In a medium-size bowl, blend biscuit mix and milk with a spoon just until dry ingredients are dampened. Drop dough into 6 mounds on baking sheet, allowing room for spreading. Bake 10 to 15 minutes or until biscuits are golden brown. Serve with hot turkey mixture.

Turkey Divan

Turkey and broccoli are smothered in a delightful creamy cheese sauce.

1 pound fresh broccoli, steamed, florets cut into lengthwise slices
1 (10-3/4-ounce) can cream of mushroom soup
1 tablespoon fresh lemon juice

Dash of Worcestershire sauce
1/4 teaspoon freshly grated nutmeg
1/2 cup freshly grated Parmesan cheese
2 cups chopped cooked turkey

Preheat oven to 300°F (150°C). Grease a shallow baking dish. Arrange broccoli in baking dish. Mix soup, lemon juice, Worcestershire sauce, and nutmeg together in a bowl. Pour half of this mixture over broccoli. Sprinkle 2 tablespoons of the Parmesan cheese over the mixture. Arrange the chopped turkey on top and pour the remaining sauce mixture over all. Sprinkle with remaining Parmesan cheese. Bake 30 minutes or until bubbly. Makes 6 servings.

Shepherd's Pie

This savory pie can be made with leftover vegetables as well as leftover meat. Traditionally made with beef, lamb, or pork, this dish can easily be made with leftover turkey. It's topped with a generous layer of hot fluffy mashed potatoes, then baked until potatoes are browned.

6 tablespoons butter or margarine

1 large onion, cut into 12 slices

3 cups chopped cooked vegetables such as carrots, cauliflower, or peas

1 cup finely chopped celery with leaves

3 cups diced cooked turkey

3 tablespoons all-purpose flour

2 cups Turkey Stock (page 2) or chicken broth

4 cups hot mashed potatoes

Preheat oven to 425°F (220°C). Melt 3 tablespoons of the butter in a medium-size skillet over medium heat. Add onion and cook until tender. Combine cooked vegetables, celery, and turkey in a 2-quart casserole dish. Cover with cooked onion slices.

Add flour to the remaining butter in the skillet and cook, stirring constantly, until lightly browned. Stir in stock and cook, stirring constantly, about 5 minutes, until mixture thickens. Pour over turkey mixture.

Spread mashed potatoes evenly over turkey mixture. Melt remaining butter and brush melted butter over potatoes. Bake about 25 minutes or until potatoes are browned. Makes 8 servings.

Deep-Dish Turkey Pie

Always a favorite in our house, it's even better the next day for lunch, if there's any left.

5 tablespoons butter or margarine
1 medium-size onion, diced
1/4 pound mushrooms, sliced
1/2 cup all-purpose flour
2-1/2 cups milk
1 teaspoon salt
1/4 teaspoon freshly ground pepper
1 chicken bouillon cube

1 cup water
3 cups cubed cooked turkey
1 cup sliced cooked carrots
1 cup cubed cooked potatoes
1 cup frozen green peas, thawed
1/2 (10- to 11-ounce) package pie crust mix
1 egg, beaten

Preheat oven to 375°F (190°C). Melt butter in a 4-quart saucepan over medium heat. Add onion and mushrooms, and cook until tender, about 5 minutes. Stir in flour and cook, stirring constantly, 1 minute. Gradually stir in milk, salt, pepper, bouillon cube, and water. Cook, stirring constantly, until mixture thickens slightly. Stir in turkey, carrots, potatoes, and peas. Spoon mixture into a 13″ × 9″ baking dish.

Prepare pie crust mix according to package directions. On a lightly floured surface, roll out dough into a 15″ × 11″ rectangle. With a knife cut out a 6″ × 3″ rectangle from center of pastry and set aside. Place large piece of pastry loosely over turkey mixture and tuck any overlapping dough under. Press gently around rim of dish to make a scalloped edge.

From the reserved pastry piece, cut out small decorative designs. Lightly brush crust with beaten egg and brush cutout designs with the remaining egg mixture. Arrange cutouts on the pie; press lightly to affix.

Bake 45 minutes or until crust is a golden brown. Put some foil around the edges of the crust if it browns too quickly. Makes 6 to 8 servings.

Homemade Ravioli with Turkey Filling & Ricotta Sauce

This recipe was handed down to me by our close friend and neighbor from Italy. She was always cooking something wonderful, and fabulous smells floated from her kitchen window.

2 cups finely chopped cooked turkey
1 egg
1/2 cup freshly grated Parmesan cheese
1 tablespoon minced parsley
1 cup finely chopped cooked spinach
Salt and freshly ground pepper to taste
Pasta Dough (see below)
Ricotta Sauce (see opposite)

Pasta Dough

4 cups all-purpose flour, sifted
1/2 teaspoon salt
5 eggs
1/4 cup warm water

Ricotta Sauce

1/4 cup olive oil
1 medium-size onion, chopped
1 pound ricotta cheese
1 cup tomato puree
1/2 cup tomato paste
1 bay leaf
1-1/2 cups water
Salt and freshly ground pepper to taste

Combine turkey, egg, Parmesan cheese, parsley, spinach, salt, and pepper in a large bowl. Cover and refrigerate until needed for filling. Prepare dough. While dough is resting, start sauce.

On a lightly floured board, roll out one ball of dough to a thickness of 1/8 inch. Cut into 2-inch squares or rounds and place a teaspoon of the turkey mixture in the center of half the squares. Cover with another unfilled square and press edges together with a fork or your fingers, making sure that the edges are sealed. Repeat with remaining dough and filling.

Cook ravioli in boiling salted water until ravioli float to the top and are tender, 6 to 8 minutes. Drain ravioli and spoon into a serving bowl. Pour hot sauce over ravioli and serve.

Pasta Dough

Add flour to a large bowl and make a well in the center. Add salt, eggs, and water to well. Stir until dough forms a ball. Knead dough on a lightly floured surface 2 minutes. Shape into 4 equal balls, cover, and let rest 10 minutes.

Ricotta Sauce

Heat olive oil in a large skillet over medium heat. Add onion and cook until onion is tender and golden brown. Add ricotta cheese, tomato puree, tomato paste, bay leaf, and water, and mix thoroughly. Season with salt and pepper. Cover and simmer, stirring occasionally, 1 hour. Makes 6 to 8 servings.

Turkey Enchiladas

Another favorite dish made with leftover turkey.

1/3 cup plus 2 tablespoons vegetable oil
2 large garlic cloves, minced
2 (4-ounce) cans chopped green chiles, drained
2 (8-ounce) cans Mexican-style stewed tomatoes,
   drained and chopped
2 cups chopped onions
2 teaspoons salt, or to taste

1/2 teaspoon dried oregano
1/2 cup Turkey Stock (page 2) or chicken broth
3 cups shredded cooked turkey
2 cups sour cream
2 cups (8 ounces) shredded Cheddar cheese
12 corn tortillas

Preheat oven to 350°F (175°C). In a large skillet, heat 2 tablespoons oil over medium heat. Add garlic, chiles, tomatoes, onions, 1 teaspoon salt, oregano, and stock. Simmer, uncovered, about 30 minutes or until thickened slightly. Set aside. In a large bowl, combine the turkey, sour cream, 1-1/2 cups of the cheese, and remaining 1 teaspoon salt.

In a large skillet, heat the remaining 1/3 cup of oil over medium heat. Using tongs, dip tortillas, one at a time, in the hot oil. Cook just until they become limp, about 1 minute. With tongs, lift out tortillas and drain on paper towels. Fill tortillas equally with turkey mixture. Roll up and arrange them with seam sides facing down in a large shallow lightly greased baking pan.

Pour the chile sauce over the enchiladas and bake until heated through, about 20 minutes. Top with remaining Cheddar cheese and return to oven until cheese melts. Makes 6 servings.

Turkey Hash

This dish is one of my favorites. I love to serve this to guests for breakfast.
We all sit down to hash with poached eggs and a cup of Earl Grey tea.
Serve with lots of toast so as not to miss a drop of the sauce.

2 cups chopped cooked turkey
2 cups chopped cooked potatoes
1 teaspoon salt
1/8 teaspoon freshly ground pepper

2 tablespoons butter or margarine
1/2 cup half-and-half
4 to 6 eggs

Combine turkey and potatoes in a bowl and season with salt and pepper. Melt butter in a large skillet over medium heat. Add turkey and potato mixture. Cook about 5 minutes or until the mixture is browned. Add half-and-half to hash and cook until it is absorbed.

Meanwhile, poach eggs: Bring about 2 inches of water to a boil in a large skillet. Reduce heat so water barely simmers. Break each egg in a cup and add to skillet. Cover and cook 3 to 5 minutes or until desired doneness. Remove eggs with a slotted spoon and drain (in spoon) on paper towels. Top each hash serving with a poached egg. Makes 4 to 6 servings.

Hot Turkey Sandwich

The best! I remember this as a kid when we would pull over at truck stops on the road,
and every time, without fail I would order the Hot Turkey, Truck-Stop Special.
It's got to be made with white bread, leftover sliced turkey breast, whipped mashed potatoes,
and lots of turkey gravy. Thanks, Jane, for your truck-stop special.
For a true truck-stop touch, serve with cooked carrots and peas.

1 cup Basic Turkey Gravy (page 97)
10 slices (1/8-inch-thick) turkey breast

4 slices white bread
2 cups hot mashed potatoes

Heat gravy in a large skillet. Arrange turkey slices in the pan without overlapping. Simmer turkey slices until heated through, 3 to 5 minutes.

Arrange 2 bread slices on each of 2 warmed plates. Using a spatula, transfer half of turkey to bread on each plate. Spoon 1 cup mashed potatoes on top of each serving of turkey, so that it is evenly spread over the turkey and bread slices. Top with 1/2 cup or more hot gravy and serve. Makes 2 servings.

Turkey & Asparagus Pasta Salad

This is a fabulous lunch to serve guests. It has tricolor spiral pasta with a Dijon mustard sauce that brings out the flavor of the asparagus and pasta.

1 cup mayonnaise
2 tablespoons Dijon mustard
2 tablespoons fresh lemon juice
6 ounces tricolor spiral or twist pasta, cooked
2 cups small cubed cooked turkey

1 red bell pepper, seeded and cut into 1-inch squares
Salt and freshly ground pepper to taste
1 (10-ounce) package frozen chopped asparagus, thawed

In a large bowl, combine mayonnaise, mustard, lemon juice, pasta, turkey, bell pepper, salt, and pepper. Gently toss asparagus spears with salad. Cover and refrigerate 1 hour or overnight. Makes 6 servings.

California Turkey Salad

If you like avocados, then this salad with millet, avocado, bell pepper, and turkey with a light spicy lime dressing is for you. It's pure California sunshine.

1-1/2 cups cooked millet
1 (8-ounce) can whole-kernel corn, drained
1/2 cup chopped red bell pepper
1 cup chopped celery
1-1/2 tablespoons green onion with top, finely chopped
1 cup shredded cooked turkey
1 small avocado, peeled, pitted, and diced

1 tablespoon vegetable oil
1 tablespoon olive oil
2-1/2 tablespoons fresh lime juice
1/4 teaspoon grated lime peel
Salt and freshly ground pepper to taste
1/4 teaspoon celery seeds
1/8 teaspoon red (cayenne) pepper

In a large bowl, gently toss millet, corn, bell pepper, celery, green onion, turkey, and avocado until well combined.

In a small bowl, whisk together oils, lime juice, lime peel, salt, pepper, celery seeds, and cayenne. Pour lime dressing over salad and toss gently. Serve immediately. Makes 4 to 6 servings.

Melon & Turkey Salad

*This makes four heavenly servings of fresh melons, celery, turkey, and cashews
on a bed of butter lettuce with a gingery creamy dressing.*

2 cups cubed cooked turkey
1/3 cup unsalted cashews
1/2 cup chopped celery
1/4 cup chopped green onions with tops
1 cup cantaloupe balls
1 cup cubed honeydew melon
Ginger Yogurt Dressing (see opposite)
Butter leaf lettuce

Ginger Yogurt Dressing
1/4 cup plain yogurt
3 tablespoons mayonnaise
3 tablespoons fresh lime juice
3/4 teaspoon ground ginger
Salt and freshly ground pepper to taste

In a large bowl, combine turkey, cashews, celery, and green onion. Mix well. Gently stir in melon, toss gently, and set aside.

Prepare dressing. Pour dressing over turkey mixture and mix gently to coat salad with dressing. Refrigerate at least 1 hour or up to 3 hours for flavors to blend. Place 2 lettuce leaves on each of 4 plates. Mound a heaping spoonful of turkey salad mixture on lettuce. Makes 4 servings.

Ginger Yogurt Dressing
Combine all ingredients in a small bowl.

Spanish-style Turkey Potato Salad

The California-Spanish flavor is accented by a spicy salsa dressing.
Garnish this salad with tortilla chips, lime wedges, and whole red chiles.

1 to 2 tablespoons chopped, seeded jalapeño
   chile
3/4 cup chopped green onions, including tops
1/4 cup chopped cilantro
2 large tomatoes, seeded and chopped
1-1/2 teaspoons salt
1 cup mayonnaise
3 tablespoons fresh lime juice
1 teaspoon ground cumin

1 teaspoon chili powder
2 pounds cooked small red potatoes, cut into
   1/4-inch-thick slices
2 cups shredded cooked turkey
1 small yellow bell pepper, diced
1 small red bell pepper, diced
1 head Romaine lettuce, rinsed and trimmed
Lime slices, tortilla chips, small chile peppers,
   and cilantro sprigs for garnish

In a medium-size bowl, combine jalapeño chile, green onions, chopped cilantro, tomatoes, and 1 teaspoon of the salt. Mix well and set aside.

In a large bowl, combine mayonnaise, lime juice, cumin, chili powder, and remaining 1/2 teaspoon salt. Mix well and stir in potatoes, turkey, bell peppers, and half of the tomato salsa mixture. Cover and refrigerate at least 1 hour before serving.

To serve, arrange lettuce leaves on a large platter and spoon turkey salad mixture evenly on top. Spoon remaining tomato salsa mixture evenly over salad. Garnish platter with lime slices, a few tortilla chips, and red chiles. Top with cilantro sprigs. Makes 6 servings.

Note

Wear rubber gloves when chopping hot chiles to avoid irritating your hands.

Thai Turkey & Rice Salad

If you like your food a little spicy, experiment with the amount of hot chili oil or hot sesame oil used in this recipe. Remember you can always add more hot oil, but you can't remove it.

2 cups cooked white rice
2/3 cup chopped water chestnuts
1/2 cup chopped snow peas (about 16)
1 cup mung bean sprouts
1/4 cup green onions, including tops
2 cups cubed cooked turkey
2 tablespoons vegetable oil

1-1/2 tablespoons soy sauce
1 tablespoon smooth peanut butter
1 tablespoon rice vinegar
1/2 teaspoon hot sesame oil or chile oil, or to taste
2 garlic cloves, minced

In a medium-size serving bowl, toss together rice, water chestnuts, snow peas, sprouts, green onions, and turkey.

In a small bowl, combine vegetable oil, soy sauce, peanut butter, vinegar, hot sesame oil, and garlic. Pour dressing over turkey-rice mixture and toss until completely combined. Serve immediately. Makes 4 to 6 servings.

Variation

For a milder flavor, use plain sesame oil.

The Whole Bird

When a whole turkey goes into the oven something wonderful happens; this usually means friends and family are getting together, and everyone helps in the kitchen. When you sit down to eat this big bird, not only is it beautiful, it's cooked to perfection. I have written down some guidelines to help you cook your whole turkey. Remember one thing, though: cooking a whole turkey should be easy and fun and, most of all, rewarding.

Cooking a Whole Turkey

• If you've just brought your fresh turkey home, it should be in a plastic wrapping. Leave this on and store in the coldest part of the refrigerator until you are ready to stuff and cook it. Put a tray under it to catch any drips. The turkey will stay fresh in the coldest part of the refrigerator for up to two days.

• When you are ready to cook your turkey, remove the neck and giblets, rinse and set aside. Rinse the turkey well under cold running water. Pat turkey dry inside and out with paper towels. If desired, loosely stuff the turkey just before placing it in the oven. Some turkeys come with either hock locks, or a band of skin; these are for securing the legs together. If your bird doesn't have either, simply tie the drumsticks together with kitchen twine. Tuck tips of wings akimbo under the back of the turkey; this holds the neck skin in place as well as keeps the wing tips from burning. Place the turkey on a rack, and place the rack in a shallow roasting pan.

• For a more moist bird, you can rub a stick of softened butter over entire turkey, inside as well if not stuffing. Preheat your oven to 325°F (165°C), no lower. See the following turkey chart for approximate roasting times. Place a loose foil tent over the breast area, but do not cover the entire turkey with foil because this gives it a steamed taste. Place a cup of water in the bottom of roasting pan.

• Baste the turkey every 30 to 45 minutes. Lift the foil off and, using a bulb baster, evenly baste the turkey with the juices from the bottom of the pan. You may want to add 1 cup of wine, broth, apple juice, or orange juice to the pan as well; these give your turkey a special flavor. If you use a fruit juice, make sure you add water with it because they tend to burn on the bottom of the pan.

• To make sure your turkey is roasted to perfection, insert a meat thermometer in the thickest part of the thigh, making sure it does not touch the bone. If your turkey comes with a pop-up thermometer, use this only as a backup check; sometimes they are not always reliable. If you do not have a meat thermometer, an old reliable method is to stick a fork into the inner thigh; if the juices run completely clear, your turkey is done. Also if the drumstick pulls quite freely from the turkey, it's cooked. The meat thermometer should read 180°F (80°C). Remove foil for the last hour so that the turkey browns evenly all over.

• When you remove the turkey from the oven, place it on a warmed serving platter and cover with fresh foil. Remove stuffing and place in a baking dish so that you may keep it warm in the oven while you are making the gravy and finishing the vegetables. Let the turkey stand for 30 minutes before carving.

• To carve your turkey: Grasp drumstick and pull away from the bird as far as possible; the joint connecting to the leg should snap free; if not, sever joint with a knife. Cut thigh from turkey by cutting along body contour. Place drumstick and thigh on a cutting surface, and cut through connecting joint. Grasp the end of the drumstick and tilt to a convenient angle. Slice meat down drumstick on all sides. With a meat fork, hold the thigh firmly on cutting surface. Cut even slices parallel to bone. Remove half of the breast by cutting along breast bone and rib cage with a sharp knife. Place half on cutting surface. Slice evenly across grain of meat. As needed, repeat same for the other side of your turkey.

Turkey Roasting Chart at 325°F (165°C)

Whole Turkey, Unstuffed	
Weight (pounds)	Roasting time (hours)
6 to 8	2-1/4 to 3-1/4
8 to 12	3-1/4 to 4
12 to 16	4 to 4-1/2
16 to 20	4-1/2 to 5
20 to 24	5 to 5-1/2
Whole Turkey, Stuffed	
6 to 8	3 to 3-1/2
8 to 12	3-1/2 to 4-1/2
12 to 16	4-1/2 to 5-1/2
16 to 20	5-1/2 to 6-1/2
20 to 24	6-1/2 to 7

Deboned Turkey with Cognac & Allspice

This is a wonderful way to roast a turkey. It's great for a party because it is so easy to carve, and everyone will be amazed and impressed.

1 (8- to 10-pound) turkey, with giblets removed
1/8 teaspoon allspice
3 tablespoons Cognac

Salt and freshly ground pepper to taste
Stuffing (pages 84 to 88)

To debone turkey: Make a cut down back of turkey from neck to tail along back bone. Then with a small sharp knife, always cutting against bone, scrape and cut flesh from carcass down one side of turkey, pulling flesh away from bones with your fingers.

Cut through ball joints that connect wings and thighs to carcass and continue down carcass until you reach ridge of turkey breast, where skin and bone meet. Stop at this point; you must be careful here as skin is thin and easily tears.

Repeat procedure for other side of turkey, cutting against bone and not skin. Again when you arrive at ridge of breast bone, stop. Lift carcass frame and cut against ridge of breast bone to free it; be very careful and cut slowly so that you do not cut outer skin. Chop off wings at elbows, leaving upper wing bones attached.

With skin side up, arrange flesh and skin on a board. Scrape meat from thigh bone while holding onto free end of joint. When you come to end of bone, cut it free from ball joint of drumstick.

If you want your turkey roast to still look like a whole turkey, leave on drumsticks and upper wings. If you want all bones removed, chop off outside ball joints of wings and drumsticks, then scrape meat off bones from inside of turkey, pulling skin inside out. You'll have four creases in outside skin where these bones were attached. Now with pliers, pull out tendons imbedded in flesh of drumsticks.

Reserve carcass to make stock.

Spread boned turkey skin side down and season with salt, pepper, allspice, and Cognac. To stuff turkey, choose your favorite stuffing and heap stuffing in center, shaping it into a loaf. Bring turkey skin up over stuffing to enclose it completely. Sew skin in place with a needle and kitchen string, or you may secure it with skewers and string. Make 3 or 4 ties around turkey to give it a cylindrical shape.

To roast turkey: Preheat oven to 350°F (175°C). Place turkey on its side on a rack in a roasting pan. Roast 30 minutes, then turn turkey on its other side. Roast 30 minutes and turn breast side up.

Insert a meat thermometer into turkey, reduce oven temperature to 320°F (165°C), and continue to roast, basting turkey with pan juices every 30 minutes, until thermometer reads 180°F (80°C), about 3 hours total roasting time.

When turkey is done, remove thermometer and strings; set on a warmed platter. Let turkey stand about 15 minutes before carving. Makes 8 to 10 servings.

Turkey with White-Wine Cream Sauce

This turkey, unstuffed, doesn't take as long to cook. The herb mixture brings out the turkey flavor.

1 (12- to 14-pound) turkey
2 tablespoons vegetable oil
Salt and freshly ground pepper to taste
1 teaspoon dried rosemary
1 teaspoon dried sage

About 1-1/2 cups Turkey Stock (page 2) or
  chicken broth
2 tablespoons cornstarch
1/2 cup white wine
3/4 cup whipping cream

Preheat oven to 350°F (175°C). Remove giblets and save for another use. Tuck wings under back. Rub skin of turkey with vegetable oil. Combine salt, pepper, rosemary, and sage and rub mixture inside cavity and over turkey skin.

Place turkey, breast side up, on a rack in a large roasting pan. Roast 30 minutes, then loosely cover turkey with foil to prevent skin from getting too brown. Roast, basting with pan juices about every 30 minutes, 3 to 3-1/2 hours or until a meat thermometer registers 180°F (80°C). Remove foil from turkey last half hour of roasting time.

Transfer turkey to a carving board. Let stand 20 minutes before carving. Meanwhile, prepare sauce: Skim fat from pan juices. Measure juices and add enough stock to make 1-3/4 cups. Dissolve cornstarch in 1/2 cup of mixture. Combine dissolved mixture, remaining stock, wine, and cream in roasting pan, and bring to a boil over medium heat, stirring constantly and scraping up browned bits from bottom of pan. Boil 1 minute or until thickened. Taste for seasoning and add salt and pepper if needed; keep warm. Carve turkey and serve with sauce. Makes 10 to 12 servings.

Roast Turkey Halves

This is another way to cut down on roasting time, yet still cook a whole turkey.
It's also perfect for a small oven.
It is very easy to do as long as you have a heavy cleaver or knife.
An even easier way is to ask the butcher to do it for you.

1/2 cup butter or margarine, softened
4 garlic cloves, crushed
3 tablespoons chili powder

1 teaspoon salt
1 (10- to 12-pound) turkey, giblets removed

In a medium-size bowl, mix butter, garlic, chili powder, and salt until a smooth, thick paste is formed; set aside.

Preheat oven to 350°F (175°C). Rinse turkey well with cold running water, pat dry with paper towels, and place on a clean cutting surface.

Use a heavy cleaver or a sharp knife to cut down both sides of back bone through ribs. Discard back bone. Now open turkey out like a book and cut through center of breastbone. Remove and discard excess fat.

Place each turkey half in a large baking pan, skin side up. Pull skin away from breast and spread half of the butter mixture evenly over each half. Pull skin back over each half and spread remaining butter mixture over skin. Insert meat thermometers between thighs and body. Loosely cover with foil.

Roast each half, on top and bottom oven racks, basting often with pan drippings. About halfway through the roasting time, switch turkey halves between top and bottom racks. Roast about 1-1/4 hours (15 minutes per pound) or until meat thermometers read 180°F (80°C). Remove foil about 40 minutes before halves are done so that skin browns evenly. Let stand 15 minutes before carving. Makes 8 to 12 servings.

Spicy Texas Turkey with Cornbread & Green Chile Stuffing

This is a unique turkey dinner for people who like their food spicy. This recipe was developed by a friend of mine in Texas who has a flair for hot food. He rubs a spicy mixture under the skin and stuffs the turkey with a spicy cornbread stuffing. This is a tamed-down version that still has lots of zing.

1/2 cup butter or margarine, softened
4 garlic cloves, crushed
3 tablespoons chili powder
1 teaspoon salt
1 (12- to 14-pound) turkey, giblets removed, rinsed and patted dry

Cornbread & Green Chile Stuffing

2 cups finely chopped onions
2 cups chopped celery
1/2 cup butter, melted

2 (4-ounce) cans chopped mild or hot green chiles, undrained
1-1/2 teaspoons ground cumin
1/2 teaspoon dried thyme
1/2 teaspoon dried oregano
3/4 teaspoon chili powder
1 cup chopped pecans, walnuts, or almonds
3 cups coarsely crumbled cornbread
Salt and freshly ground pepper to taste
Turkey Stock (page 2) or chicken broth as needed

In a small bowl, mix together butter, garlic, chili powder, and salt to a thick paste; set aside. Prepare stuffing.

Turn turkey on its breast side, and with kitchen shears, make a cut, starting at tail and continue to cut through turkey skin all the way to the neck. Place your hand under skin, starting at tail, and lift skin away from flesh. Loosen skin around drumstick and try to get as much skin loose near breast, being very careful not to tear skin. Do other side of turkey. Turn turkey over on its back, place your hand under breast skin, and gently work skin away from flesh on both sides.

Using your fingers, get a small amount of butter mixture and rub under skin, all over front and back of turkey, making sure you get legs as well.

Loosely stuff turkey cavity with stuffing. Tuck wings under back and tie drumsticks together with kitchen string. Place turkey breast side up on a rack in a roasting pan. Make sure skin on bottom is tucked under turkey. Place a meat thermometer in thickest part of turkey thigh next to body. Place a foil tent over turkey.

Roast about 3-1/2 to 4 hours or until thermometer reads 180°F (80°C), and baste every 30 minutes. Remove foil before last 30 minutes of roasting so skin browns evenly. Transfer turkey to a carving board. Remove stuffing and place in bowl and keep warm. Let turkey stand at least 15 to 20 minutes before carving. Makes 8 to 10 servings.

Cornbread & Green Chile Stuffing

Melt butter in a large skillet over medium heat. Add onions and celery and cook until tender and onions are light golden brown. Add chiles with juice, cumin, thyme, oregano, and chili powder. Cook mixture about 3 minutes, stirring occasionally. Transfer mixture to a large bowl and add nuts, cornbread, salt and pepper to taste. Add a little stock to mixture if it is too dry. Combine stuffing and let cool.

A package of cornbread mix can be used to make the cornbread for this stuffing.

Joe-Linda's Barbecued Turkey

You used to have to go to the Silver Peso in Larkspur, California, for this melt-off-the-bone barbecued turkey. Occasionally during the summertime, Tokyo Joe would heat up coals and cook his special barbecued turkey. Now Linda and Joe have joined together to make it easy for you to have this special turkey at home. Invite plenty of friends. Thanks again, Joe, Linda, and Crisco, for this fabulous recipe.

4 teaspoons garlic powder
2 teaspoons onion powder
2 teaspoons hickory-smoked salt, or to taste
2 tablespoons Liquid Smoke flavoring
1 (12- to 14-pound) turkey, giblets removed, rinsed

3-1/2 cups cold water
3 tablespoons cornstarch
3/4 cup red wine or port
Salt and freshly ground pepper to taste

Prepare outdoor grill for direct cooking. When grill is ready, add a handful of hickory chips. In a small bowl, combine together garlic powder, onion powder, hickory salt, and Liquid Smoke. Rub mixture evenly on outside of turkey and inside cavity as well.

Pour 2 cups of the water into a large roasting pan and place seasoned turkey in roasting pan. Place pan on top of grill rack. Cover turkey with lid of roasting pan or with foil. You do not need to use grill lid. Grill lid may be used but cooking time will be 30 minutes longer.

Check turkey every 30 minutes and baste, making sure there is enough water in roasting pan; add more water as needed, keeping about 2 cups in pan. Toward the end of cooking time, let volume of water decrease to about 1 cup. Cook turkey 2-1/2 to 3 hours or until leg breaks away from body very easily. A thermometer inserted in thickest part of turkey thigh should read 180°F (80°C).

Remove roasting pan from grill. Remove turkey from pan and place turkey on a large warmed platter. Let turkey stand at least 30 minutes before carving.

While turkey is resting, make gravy: In a medium-size bowl, whisk together remaining 1-1/2 cups water and cornstarch; set aside. Skim fat from juices in roasting pan. Add cornstarch mixture to roasting pan, and bring to a boil on top of stove over medium-high heat, stirring constantly. Reduce heat to medium. Add wine and simmer just until sauce thickens, about 3 minutes. Season with salt and pepper to taste. Makes 10 to 12 servings.

Tangerine-Glazed Turkey

This is a fabulous feast. The cheesecloth keeps the turkey basted with juices, and the tangerine glaze makes this a meal to remember. Serve with Traditional English Roasties (page 95) and your favorite vegetable dish.

Apple & Apricot Sausage Stuffing (page 85)
Salt and freshly ground pepper to taste
1 (14-pound) turkey
1 cup butter, softened

1 cup vegetable oil
2 cups fresh tangerine juice (about 7 tangerines)
3 cups Turkey Stock (page 2) or chicken broth
1/4 cup all-purpose flour

Preheat oven to 425°F (205°C). Make stuffing as directed. Stuffing may be made one day in advance, but do not stuff turkey until just before cooking.

Rinse turkey inside and out with cold running water. Pat dry with paper towels. Season inside and out with salt and pepper. Pack neck cavity loosely with some of stuffing; fold neck skin under body and fasten it with a skewer. Pack inside cavity loosely with remaining stuffing and tie drumsticks together with kitchen string. Spoon any leftover stuffing into a baking dish and refrigerate. Spread turkey with 1/2 cup of the butter.

Place turkey breast side up on a rack in a large roasting pan. Roast 30 minutes. Meanwhile, in a medium-size saucepan, melt remaining 1/2 cup butter and oil together and let mixture cool.

Reduce oven temperature to 325°F (165°C). Baste turkey with pan juices. Dip cheesecloth in butter-oil mixture just until well soaked. Drape cheesecloth over turkey, making sure no cheesecloth is hanging outside of pan. Return turkey to oven.

Stir tangerine juice into remaining butter-oil mixture and set aside. Lift cheesecloth and baste turkey with tangerine mixture every 30 minutes. Bake 3 to 3-1/2 hours or until a meat thermometer inserted in thickest part of thigh reads 180°F (80°C) and juices run clear when thigh is pierced with a fork.

Discard cheesecloth and trussing string. Transfer turkey to a warmed serving platter and let stand 20 to 30 minutes. Prepare gravy, using stock and flour, according to directions for Basic Turkey Gravy (page 97). If you have extra stuffing, baste it with some of the pan juices and bake 30 minutes. Makes 8 servings.

All the Trimmings

There's nothing quite like turkey plus all the trimmings. This chapter will give you some recipe ideas for what to serve alongside that fabulous turkey you plan to cook. There are some stuffings that you may use either to stuff your turkey or to bake in a separate dish. A rather exotic one is the Middle Eastern-style Stuffing with Golden Raisins, and one of my favorites is the Apple & Apricot Sausage Stuffing, just to mention a couple.

Some wonderful vegetable side dishes include Glazed Carrots, Oven-roasted Onions, and Cauliflower au Gratin. A potato dish, Traditional English Roasties, dates back to the sixteenth century. There are some wonderful gravies, glazes, marinades, and sauces to accent your meal, and don't forget the relishes, particularly the cranberry relishes, without which I personally think any turkey meal isn't complete. So go ahead, indulge, and have turkey with all the trimmings.

Middle Eastern-style Stuffing with Golden Raisins

The couscous and golden raisins in this recipe give it a texture different from that of your usual stuffing. Serve with your favorite turkey recipe or use to stuff a turkey.

1/4 cup plus 2 tablespoons olive oil
2 cups finely chopped onions
1/2 cup finely chopped celery
2 large garlic cloves, minced
2/3 cup chopped green bell pepper
1/3 cup almonds, finely chopped
1/2 cup golden raisins
3 tablespoons chopped parsley
1/4 teaspoon ground cinnamon

1-1/2 teaspoons ground coriander
1 teaspoon ground cumin
1/4 teaspoon dried thyme
Salt and freshly ground pepper to taste
2-1/4 cups water
1 (10-ounce) box or 1-2/3 cups couscous
3/4 cup Turkey Stock (page 2) or chicken broth
2 tablespoons butter or margarine

Preheat oven to 325°F (165°C). Grease a 3- to 4-quart casserole dish. Heat 1/4 cup olive oil in a large skillet over medium-low heat. Add onions, celery, garlic, and bell pepper, and cook until vegetables are tender, about 3 minutes. Add almonds, raisins, parsley, cinnamon, coriander, cumin, thyme, salt, and pepper. Cook mixture, stirring, 1 minute. Transfer to a large bowl.

Add the water, remaining 2 tablespoons olive oil, salt, and pepper to a large saucepan and bring to a boil. Stir in couscous and remove from heat. Let couscous stand 5 minutes or until water is absorbed. Fluff couscous with a fork and add to vegetable mixture. Mix stuffing together gently, but thoroughly.

Spoon stuffing into casserole dish, drizzle it with stock, and dot with butter. Cover and bake in middle of preheated oven 30 minutes. Uncover and bake another 30 minutes. Makes 8 to 10 servings.

Variation

Omit stock and butter and do not bake. Use cooled mixture to stuff a 12- to 14-pound turkey.

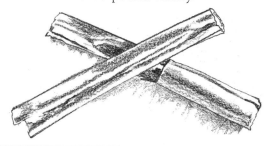

Apple & Apricot Sausage Stuffing

Use Macintosh apples for this; they truly are the best. This stuffing is wonderful on its own, but if stuffed into a turkey it seasons the turkey beautifully with just a hint of apricot.

2 cups whole-wheat bread cubes
5 cups sourdough bread cubes
1-1/2 pounds spicy turkey sausages, casing removed
1-1/2 cups chopped onions
1 cup chopped celery
1 cup chopped dried apricots

2 small Macintosh apples, cored, peeled, and chopped
1/2 cup chopped fresh parsley
1 cup Turkey Stock (page 2) or chicken broth
6 tablespoons butter or margarine, melted
2 tablespoons butter or margarine

Preheat oven to 350°F (175°C). Grease a 3- to 4-quart casserole dish. Arrange bread cubes in a large baking pan. Bake, tossing occasionally, 18 to 20 minutes or until golden brown. Transfer toasted bread to a large bowl and let cool.

In a large skillet, cook turkey sausage and onions over medium heat, stirring to break up sausage, until sausage is no longer pink. Add celery and cook 2 minutes.

Add turkey mixture to large bowl with bread. Mix in apricots, apples, and parsley and toss mixture well. Drizzle stock and melted butter over stuffing and mix well. Spoon stuffing into casserole dish and dot with pieces of remaining butter. Bake, covered, 30 minutes. Uncover and bake another 30 minutes. Makes 8 to 10 servings.

Variation

Omit stock and solid butter and do not bake. Use cooled mixture to stuff a 12- to 14-pound turkey.

Rice Stuffing with Figs & Allspice

I often use this mixture to stuff turkey legs or a small turkey.

4 tablespoons butter
1/2 cup pine nuts
1 onion, minced
1 tablespoon allspice

1-1/4 cups cooked rice
1-3/4 cups Turkey Stock (page 2) or chicken
  broth
3/4 cup chopped dried figs

Preheat oven to 350°F (175°C). Grease a 2-quart casserole dish. Melt 2 tablespoons of the butter in a large skillet over medium heat. Add pine nuts and cook, stirring occasionally, until lightly browned, about 4 minutes. Add onion and cook until soft, about 2 minutes. Stir in allspice and rice. Add stock and bring to a boil. Cover and simmer 15 minutes. Add figs and simmer another 10 minutes. Spoon stuffing into casserole dish and dot with pieces of remaining butter. Bake 30 minutes. Makes 4 to 6 servings.

Variation

Omit 2 tablespoons of the butter and do not bake. Use cooled mixture to stuff an 8- to 10-pound turkey.

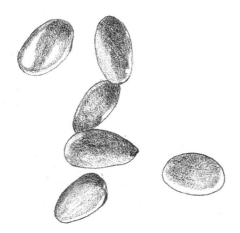

Mashed Potato & Apple Stuffing

Great as a side dish, use Granny Smith apples for this one.

6 tablespoons butter
2 cups chopped celery
2 cups chopped onions
2 Granny Smith apples, cored, peeled, and
    finely chopped
1 tablespoon cider vinegar
1/2 teaspoon dried sage

1-1/2 teaspoons Italian seasoning
1/4 cup chopped fresh parsley
4 russet potatoes, peeled, cooked, and mashed
1/4 cup milk, heated until hot
Salt and freshly ground pepper to taste
5 cups toasted white bread cubes
1/3 cup Turkey Stock (page 2) or chicken broth

Preheat oven to 325°F (165°C). Grease a 3- to 4-quart casserole dish. Melt 2 tablespoons of the butter in a large skillet over medium-low heat. Add celery and onions, and cook until tender. Add apples and cook just until apples are tender, about 4 minutes. Stir in vinegar, sage, Italian seasoning, and parsley, and cook 3 minutes.

In a large bowl, mix together mashed potatoes, milk, 2 tablespoons of the butter, salt, and pepper until mixture is well blended and smooth. Add apple mixture, toasted bread cubes, salt, and pepper, and mix well.

Spoon stuffing into casserole dish, drizzle with stock, and dot with remaining butter. Cover and bake 30 minutes. Remove cover and bake another 30 minutes. Makes 8 to 10 servings.

Variation

Omit stock and 2 tablespoons of the butter and do not bake. Use cooled mixture to stuff a 12- to 14-pound turkey.

Oyster & Lemon Stuffing

Some people don't like oysters in their stuffing, or even next to it for that matter.
But if you are like me and love oysters, here is a stuffing done with rye bread, capers,
and lemon juice that is sure to please.

1 cup chopped oysters, liquor reserved

4 cups toasted dark or light rye bread crumbs

1/4 cup butter or margarine, melted

1 teaspoon chopped capers

1/4 cup fresh lemon juice

2 tablespoons chopped sweet pickle

2 teaspoons salt, or to taste

Freshly ground pepper

1/2 cup Turkey Stock (page 2) or chicken broth

Preheat oven to 350°F (175°C). Grease a 2-quart casserole dish. Mix together oysters, bread crumbs, butter, capers, lemon juice, pickle, salt, pepper, and stock. If stuffing seems too dry, add enough of the oyster liquor or water just to moisten.

Spoon into casserole dish, drizzle with stock, and dot with remaining butter. Cover and bake 30 minutes. Remove cover and bake another 30 minutes. Makes 4 to 6 servings.

Variation

Do not bake. Use cooled mixture to stuff an 8- to 10-pound turkey.

Southwestern Cornbread

Cut cornbread into squares and serve as a side dish with any of the grilled turkey dishes.

12 ounces chorizo
2 cups yellow cornmeal
2 teaspoons salt
2 teaspoons baking powder
1 teaspoon baking soda
2 cups buttermilk
4 large eggs, slightly beaten

1/2 cup butter or margarine, melted
2 cups canned cream-style corn
2 cups (8 ounces) shredded Monterey Jack
   cheese with chiles
2 (4-ounce) cans diced green chiles, drained
2 small onions, grated
1/2 cup cilantro

Preheat oven to 350°F (175°C). Grease 2 (10-inch) cast-iron skillets or a large shallow baking dish. In a small skillet, cook sausage, turning occasionally, until browned on all sides. Cool slightly and cut into 1/4-inch-thick slices. In a medium-size bowl, stir together cornmeal, salt, baking powder, and baking soda.

In a large bowl, stir together sausage, buttermilk, eggs, butter, corn, cheese, chiles, onions, and cilantro. Add cornmeal mixture and mix well. Pour batter into greased pans. Bake about 40 minutes or until cornbread is golden brown and a wooden pick inserted in center comes out clean. Makes 6 to 8 servings.

Oven-roasted Onions

These onions are thickly sliced and roasted with brown sugar. They just melt in your mouth.

3 tablespoons olive oil
4 (about 1-1/4 pounds) onions
1-1/2 teaspoons salt

2 tablespoons light brown sugar
1 tablespoon cider vinegar
Parsley sprigs

Preheat oven to 400°F (205°C). Grease 2 (15″ × 10″) baking pans with 1 tablespoon of the olive oil. Cut onions crosswise into 3/4-inch-thick slices. Place onion slices in a single layer in pans. In a cup, mix remaining olive oil with 1 teaspoon salt. Brush onion slices with half of the oil mixture. Bake 45 minutes.

With a spatula, turn onion slices over; brush with remaining oil mixture. Switch pans between upper and lower racks, and bake onions 30 minutes.

In a cup, mix together brown sugar, vinegar, and remaining 1/2 teaspoon salt. Brush onion slices with brown sugar mixture and bake another 5 minutes or until onions are tender and golden. Use spatula to remove onion slices, and turn them onto a warmed platter. Garnish with fresh parsley. Makes 12 servings.

Sliced Cheesy Baked Potatoes

I grew up eating these potatoes. When I was a kid, we would get the biggest russets we could find, and sometimes, I would have one of these potatoes as my dinner on its own.

4 medium-size russet potatoes
1 teaspoon salt
3 tablespoons butter or margarine, melted
1/2 teaspoon dried parsley
1/2 teaspoon dried thyme

1/2 teaspoon dried chives
Dash of paprika
1/4 cup (1 ounce) shredded Cheddar cheese
1-1/2 teaspoons freshly grated Parmesan
 cheese

Preheat oven to 400°F (205°C). Scrub potatoes well. Cut potatoes as if making 1/4-inch-thick slices but without cutting all the way through. Put potatoes in a baking pan and fan slices slightly. Sprinkle each potato with salt, drizzle with butter, and sprinkle with herbs. Bake potatoes about 50 minutes. Remove from oven and sprinkle with cheeses. Bake another 10 minutes or until cheeses melt and potatoes are soft inside. Makes 4 servings.

Summary Squash Casserole

This is down-home cooking at its best; a friend of mine from North Carolina gave me this recipe.

4 cups sliced summer squash
1 cup chopped onion
1 cup chopped green bell pepper
1/4 cup butter, softened

1/2 cup coarsely crushed crackers
2 eggs, slightly beaten
Salt and freshly ground pepper to taste
1/2 cup (2 ounces) shredded Cheddar cheese

Preheat oven to 350°F (175°C). Grease a 1-quart casserole dish. Steam squash, onion, and bell pepper over boiling water until tender, about 10 minutes. Transfer vegetables to a large bowl; stir in butter, crackers, eggs, salt, and pepper. Transfer mixture to prepared casserole dish. Sprinkle with Cheddar cheese and bake 45 minutes or until browned and casserole is firm when pressed with fingertips. Makes 4 servings.

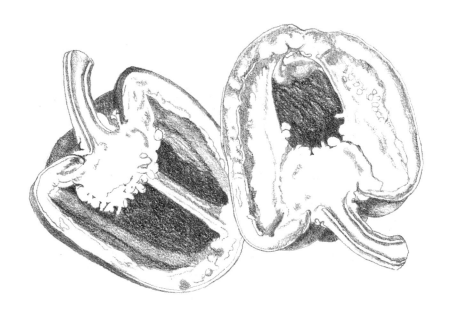

Brussels Sprouts with Bacon & Onions

If you like Brussels sprouts with your turkey, you'll love this recipe.

1/2 teaspoon salt, or to taste
2 pounds Brussels sprouts, trimmed
6 thick bacon slices
2 small onions, diced

6 tablespoons butter or margarine
Freshly ground pepper to taste
2 tablespoons cider vinegar

In a large pot, bring 2 cups water and salt to a boil. Add Brussels sprouts and boil just until tender, about 8 minutes. Drain and cool sprouts by running cold water over them. Cut each sprout in half through stem end; set aside.

Heat a medium-size skillet over medium heat. Add bacon slices and fry until golden brown, about 3 minutes. Drain bacon on paper towels and crumble. Pour off all but 3 tablespoons of bacon fat. Add onions to skillet and cook over medium heat until soft, about 5 minutes. Remove onions with a slotted spoon and set aside.

Pour out fat and wipe skillet. Add butter to skillet and melt over medium heat. Add Brussels sprouts and cook until lightly browned, about 10 minutes. Add bacon and onions. Season with freshly ground pepper and salt. Lightly sprinkle with vinegar and heat through. Serve hot. Makes 8 servings.

Sweet Potato Casserole

I love the smell of the sweet potatoes, honey, and nutmeg baking in the oven.

4 pounds sweet potatoes, peeled and cut
   crosswise into thirds
5 tablespoons butter or margarine
1 pound carrots, peeled and thinly sliced
1 small onion, chopped
1-1/2 tablespoons water
1/2 cup honey

1 garlic clove, halved
1-1/2 cups whipping cream
2 large eggs
1/4 teaspoon salt
Freshly ground pepper to taste
Pinch of freshly grated nutmeg

Preheat oven to 375°F (190°C). In a large pot, bring 2 cups water to a boil. Add potatoes and cook over medium heat until about half cooked, about 20 minutes. Drain and let cool before handling potatoes.

Melt 4 tablespoons of the butter in a medium-size saucepan over medium heat. Add carrots and onion, and toss to coat with butter. Stir in water and honey. Increase heat to high and cook, stirring frequently, until glazed, 5 to 7 minutes. Remove from heat and set aside. Rub a large gratin dish with garlic halves and discard garlic. Butter dish with 1/2 tablespoon of the butter.

Cut sweet potatoes into 1/4-inch-thick slices. Layer half the potatoes in dish. Top evenly with all of carrot mixture, then layer remaining potatoes over carrots. In a medium-size bowl, whisk together cream, eggs, salt, pepper, and nutmeg until blended. Pour over vegetables. Dot with remaining 1/2 tablespoon butter. Bake about 25 minutes or until egg mixture is set. Let stand 10 minutes before serving. Makes 8 servings.

Traditional English Roasties

This is a favorite in our house; we have these potatoes with just about everything. The secret to these potatoes is to let potatoes stop steaming after they have been boiled and before baking. They are crispy on the outside and soft in the middle.

2 cups water
1 chicken bouillon cube

4 medium-size russet potatoes, peeled
2 tablespoons vegetable oil

Preheat oven to 350°F (175°C). Grease a baking dish large enough to hold potatoes without crowding. In a large pot over medium heat, bring the water and bouillon cube to a boil and boil 3 minutes or until cube dissolves. Add potatoes and bring back to a boil. Reduce heat and simmer, covered, 15 minutes or until a layer of potato lifts slightly. Remove potatoes with a slotted spoon and transfer them to prepared baking dish.

Let steam on potatoes evaporate, turn over, and let steam evaporate on this side as well. Drizzle oil over potatoes.

Bake 30 minutes, brush with oil in pan, and turn over. Bake another 30 minutes or until potatoes are golden brown and crisp on outside. Serve hot. Makes 4 servings.

Variation

Potatoes can be baked in pan with a roast. Add them at the beginning of the last hour of baking time and baste with pan juices.

Glazed Carrots

Simple yet very tasty, these accompany turkey so well.

2 bunches baby carrots, scrubbed and trimmed
1/3 cup light brown sugar

2 tablespoons butter
Parsley sprigs

Steam carrots over boiling water just until tender, about 10 minutes. In a large saucepan, cook brown sugar and butter over medium heat, stirring constantly, until sugar dissolves. Add steamed carrots and cook, turning carrots, until they are thoroughly glazed and tender, about 12 minutes. Garnish with parsley sprigs. Makes 4 to 6 servings.

Cauliflower au Gratin

You can put this delicious dish together in no time.

1 medium-size cauliflower head
2 teaspoons prepared mustard
1/2 teaspoon salt

3/4 cup mayonnaise
3/4 cup (3 ounces) shredded Cheddar cheese
Paprika

Preheat oven to 325°F (165°C). Grease a 1-quart casserole dish. Cut cauliflower in half. Steam over boiling water until just tender, about 10 minutes. Break into florets and place in prepared dish.

In a small bowl, mix mustard, salt, and mayonnaise; spread evenly over cauliflower. Top with Cheddar cheese and bake until cheese is melted, about 5 minutes. Sprinkle with paprika and serve. Makes 4 servings.

Basic Turkey Gravy

*Always a favorite, this basic gravy should be made from the pan juices after roasting a turkey;
it just seems to taste better that way. It's even better served the next day
with your Hot Turkey Sandwich (page 64).*

Pan juices from roasted turkey
About 4 cups Turkey Stock (page 2) or chicken
   broth
1/2 cup white wine

6 tablespoons all-purpose flour
1/2 cup whipping cream
Salt and freshly ground pepper to taste
Finely chopped cooked turkey giblets (optional)

Strain pan juices, skim off fat from juices, and set aside. Reserve 6 tablespoons of the fat. Measure juices and add enough stock to make 4 cups; set aside.

Add wine to turkey roasting pan and heat on top of stove over high heat, scraping up browned bits that cling to pan. Boil liquid until reduced by half, about 3 minutes, and reserve.

In a large saucepan, combine reserved fat and flour; cook over medium heat, stirring constantly, about 3 minutes. Whisk in wine mixture from pan and stock. Bring to a boil, stirring constantly. Reduce heat and simmer about 5 minutes or until gravy has thickened. Stir in cream and heat through. Season with salt and pepper. Add giblets to gravy, if desired. Serve hot. Makes about 3 cups

Favorite Barbecue Sauce

This sauce is proof that a committee of six in the kitchen can create something that is an instant success. A versatile sauce, it goes great with barbecued turkey drumsticks, thighs, or even a grilled turkey breast. It's also good in baked beans.

2 cups domestic beer
3 tablespoons Worcestershire sauce
1 cup ketchup
2 tablespoons light brown sugar
2 teaspoons Liquid Smoke flavoring
2 tablespoons fresh lemon juice
1 tablespoon butter

1/2 cup grated onion
1/2 teaspoon red (cayenne) pepper, or to taste
2 teaspoons garlic powder
1 teaspoon ground cumin
2 teaspoons prepared mustard
1 bay leaf

In a large saucepan, combine all ingredients. Simmer, covered, 30 minutes, stirring occasionally. Use as a basting sauce for grilled turkey. Makes about 4-1/2 cups.

Note

Any leftover sauce used to baste raw or partially cooked turkey must be brought to a boil before serving with cooked turkey.

White Wine & Garlic Sauce

Use the juices from the pan of the turkey you are cooking; this is a delightful turkey gravy.

Pan juices from roasted turkey
About 1 cup Turkey Stock (page 2) or chicken
   broth
1/2 cup white wine
2 garlic cloves, minced

2 tablespoons cornstarch dissolved in 2
   tablespoons water
1 tablespoon chopped parsley
Salt and freshly ground pepper to taste

Strain pan juices; skim off fat from juices and set aside. Measure juices and add enough stock to make 1 cup; set aside.

Add wine and garlic to turkey roasting pan and heat on top of stove over high heat, scraping up browned bits that cling to pan. Boil liquid until reduced by half, about 3 minutes; reserve.

In a large saucepan, combine stock mixture, cornstarch mixture, and reduced wine mixture. Bring to a boil, stirring constantly. Reduce heat and simmer about 5 minutes or until gravy has thickened. Add parsley, salt, and pepper. Serve hot. Makes about 1 cup.

Pineapple-Ginger Sauce

Use this sauce as a marinade for turkey or as a basting sauce for grilled turkey.

1 cup pineapple juice
1/4 cup soy sauce
1/4 cup cider vinegar

1/4 cup vegetable oil
1/2 teaspoon ground ginger
1 tablespoon light brown sugar

In a medium-size bowl, combine all ingredients. Use as a basting sauce or marinate uncooked turkey in mixture for 1 hour before cooking. Makes about 1-3/4 cups.

Double-Orange Sherry Glaze

A double burst of orange flavor accented with sherry.

1/2 cup frozen concentrated orange juice,
   thawed

1/4 cup orange marmalade
3 tablespoons dry sherry

In a small saucepan over medium-low heat, combine all ingredients. Cook, stirring constantly, until marmalade melts and mixture is blended. Cool and use as a basting sauce for turkey during the last half hour of grilling. Makes about 3/4 cup.

Hot Mango Chutney

Enjoy this alongside any of the curried turkey recipes.

1 slightly unripe mango, peeled and cut into
   1/8-inch cubes
2 jalapeño chiles, seeded and chopped

3 garlic cloves, finely chopped
2 teaspoons olive oil
Salt to taste

In a medium-size bowl, combine all ingredients. Cover and refrigerate 1 hour before serving. Makes 1 cup.

Cranberry-Tomato Relish in Lemon Cups

This dish adds a delicious festive touch to roasted turkey.

5 lemons
1 (28-ounce) can tomatoes, chopped, with liquid
  reserved
1 large onion, finely chopped

1 cup sugar
2 tablespoons minced gingerroot
1 (12-ounce) package cranberries

Halve lemons, juice, and remove all pulp and membranes. If desired, cut edges with scissors or a knife to make a zigzag effect. Trim a thin slice from each bottom so each half sits upright.

In a large saucepan, combine 1/2 cup of the lemon juice, chopped tomatoes and their juice, onion, sugar, and gingerroot. Bring to a boil over medium-high heat, stirring occasionally. Reduce heat and simmer 20 minutes. Add cranberries and cook, stirring occasionally, until reduced to about 3-1/2 cups, about 30 minutes. To avoid scorching, stir more often as mixture thickens. Cool and divide evenly among lemon cups. Makes about 8 servings.

Notes

Reserve remaining lemon juice for another use.

Orange cups can be prepared in the same manner as lemon cups. Use small or large oranges, depending on their filling.

Cranberry-Pear Relish

Here's a crunchy, uncooked cranberry relish that is sure to please everyone.
Spoon relish into decorative lemon or orange cups (see page 101), if desired.

1 large orange, unpeeled, cut into 8 pieces, and
  seeded
1 (12-ounce) package fresh cranberries
1 cup pitted prunes
1/2 cup chopped walnuts

1/2 cup sugar
1 tablespoon grated gingerroot
1 (16-ounce) can pear halves, drained and
  diced

In a food processor with steel blade, process orange, cranberries, prunes, walnuts, sugar, and gingerroot until coarsely chopped. Pour mixture into a large bowl and stir in pears. Cover and refrigerate 1 hour. Serve chilled or at room temperature. Makes 6 cups.

Metric Conversion Charts

Comparison to Metric Measure				
When You Know	Symbol	Multiply By	To Find	Symbol
teaspoons	tsp	5.0	milliliters	ml
tablespoons	tbsp	15.0	milliliters	ml
fluid ounces	fl. oz.	30.0	milliliters	ml
cups	c	0.24	liters	l
pints	pt.	0.47	liters	l
quarts	qt.	0.95	liters	l
ounces	oz.	28.0	grams	g
pounds	lb.	0.45	kilograms	kg
Fahrenheit	F	5/9 (after subtracting 32)	Celsius	C

Liquid Measure to Milliliters		
1/4 teaspoon	=	1.25 milliliters
1/2 teaspoon	=	2.5 milliliters
3/4 teaspoon	=	3.75 milliliters
1 teaspoon	=	5.0 milliliters
1-1/4 teaspoons	=	6.25 milliliters
1-1/2 teaspoons	=	7.5 milliliters
1-3/4 teaspoons	=	8.75 milliliters
2 teaspoons	=	10.0 milliliters
1 tablespoon	=	15.0 milliliters
2 tablespoons	=	30.0 milliliters

Fahrenheit to Celsius	
F	C
200–205	95
220–225	105
245–250	120
275	135
300–305	150
325–330	165
345–350	175
370–375	190
400–405	205
425–430	220
445–450	230
470–475	245
500	260

Liquid Measure to Liters		
1/4 cup	=	0.06 liters
1/2 cup	=	0.12 liters
3/4 cup	=	0.18 liters
1 cup	=	0.24 liters
1-1/4 cups	=	0.3 liters
1-1/2 cups	=	0.36 liters
2 cups	=	0.48 liters
2-1/2 cups	=	0.6 liters
3 cups	=	0.72 liters
3-1/2 cups	=	0.84 liters
4 cups	=	0.96 liters
4-1/2 cups	=	1.08 liters
5 cups	=	1.2 liters
5-1/2 cups	=	1.32 liters

Index

About the Author

Franki Papai Secunda was born in Encino, California. Her dad made movies and developed America's favorite nearsighted cartoon star, Mr. Magoo. Franki did her first television commercial when she was three and a half years old. Franki studied and taught dance for several years. She is a successful songwriter as well as a freelance writer.

Her love for writing and cooking makes it very easy for her to come up with great recipes that she likes to share with family and friends. In addition, she has catered banquets, private parties and even romantic dinners for two.

She is also the author of *The Catlover's Cookbook*, which contains recipes for cats. A cat lover, she dedicated the book to Roxy, a very special blue-point friend.